Devil's Advocates

DEVIL'S ADVOCATES is a series of books devoted to exploring the classics of horror cinema. Contributors to the series come from the fields of teaching, academia, journalism and fiction, but all have one thing in common: a passion for the horror film and a desire to share it with the widest possible audience.

'The admirable Devil's Advocates series is not only essential – and fun – reading for the serious horror fan but should be set texts on any genre course.'
Dr Ian Hunter, Reader in Film Studies, De Montfort University, Leicester

'Auteur Publishing's new Devil's Advocates critiques on individual titles... offer bracingly fresh perspectives from passionate writers. The series will perfectly complement the BFI archive volumes.' **Christopher Fowler,** *Independent on Sunday*

'Devil's Advocates has proven itself more than capable of producing impassioned, intelligent analyses of genre cinema... quickly becoming the go-to guys for intelligent, easily digestible film criticism.' ***Horror Talk.com***

'Auteur Publishing continue the good work of giving serious critical attention to significant horror films.' ***Black Static***

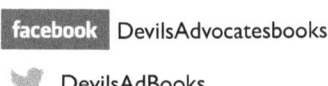

DevilsAdvocatesbooks

DevilsAdBooks

ALSO AVAILABLE IN THIS SERIES

Antichrist Amy Simmons

Black Sunday Martyn Conterio

The Blair Witch Project Peter Turner

Candyman Jon Towlson

Cannibal Holocaust Calum Waddell

Carrie Neil Mitchell

The Company of Wolves James Gracey

Creepshow Simon Brown

The Curse of Frankenstein Marcus K. Harmes

Dead of Night Jez Conolly & David Bates

The Descent James Marriot

The Devils Darren Arnold

Don't Look Now Jessica Gildersleeve

The Fly Emma Westwood

Frenzy Ian Cooper

Halloween Murray Leeder

House of Usher Evert Jan van Leeuwen

In the Mouth of Madness Michael Blyth

It Follows Joshua Grimm

Ju-on The Grudge Marisa Hayes

Let the Right One In Anne Billson

M Samm Deighan

The Mummy Doris V. Sutherland

Macbeth Rebekah Owens

Nosferatu Cristina Massaccesi

Saw Benjamin Poole

Scream Steven West

The Shining Laura Mee

The Silence of the Lambs Barry Forshaw

Suspiria Alexandra Heller-Nicholas

The Texas Chain Saw Massacre James Rose

The Thing Jez Conolly

Twin Peaks: Fire Walk With Me Lindsay Hallam

Witchfinder General Ian Cooper

FORTHCOMING

Blood and Black Lace Roberto Curti

Daughters of Darkness Kat Ellinger

Peeping Tom Kiri Walden

[REC] Jim Harper

Devil's Advocates

Shivers

Luke Aspell

Acknowledgements

Thanks to John Atkinson at Auteur. Thanks to my 'focus group': Sarah Currant and her colleagues at the BFI Reuben Library, Selina Parker and Steven Perdue at the BFI Bookshop. Thanks to Simon Payne and Deniz Johns. Thanks to Alexandra Heller-Nicholas. Thanks to Bali Beskin at the Atlantis Bookshop.

First published in 2019 by
Auteur, 24 Hartwell Crescent, Leighton Buzzard LU7 1NP
www.auteur.co.uk
Copyright © Auteur 2019

Series design: Nikki Hamlett at Cassels Design
Set by Cassels Design www.casselsdesign.co.uk

All rights reserved. No part of this publication may be reproduced in any material form (including photocopying or storing in any medium by electronic means and whether or not transiently or incidentally to some other use of this publication) without the permission of the copyright owner.

British Library Cataloguing-in-Publication Data
A catalogue record for this book is available from the British Library

ISBN paperback: 978-1-911325-97-0
ISBN ebook: 978-1-911325-98-7

Contents

First Reel 7

Second Reel 29

Third Reel 47

Fourth Reel 77

Fifth Reel 93

If you have to construct something you can make a garage out of it or you can make a cathedral out of it. We use the same means, the same structural methods for all these things. - Mies van der Rohe.[1]

First Reel

1 – Starliner Tower in Merrick's first slide

A photograph of a tower block. The photograph speaks. We are watching a tape-and-slides presentation for prospective residents of Starliner Tower apartments.[2] Northrop Frye suggested that Canadian literature evinced a 'garrison mentality',[3] concerned always to preserve itself from external threats; a short drive from 'downtown Montreal', Starliner Tower takes this to its furthest extreme – a self-contained luxury apartment complex that offers its residents the dream of escaping from the planet altogether. The melodious, caressive voice of Ronald Merrick (Ronald Mlodzik), which may trigger ASMR in those susceptible to it, invites us to 'cruise the seasons, the sun and the stars without ever leaving the great ship Starliner'. This opening sequence resumes, in condensed form, the use of pastiche found in Cronenberg's first two feature-length films. Merrick's promotional spiel belongs to a more audience-friendly genre of discourse than the detailed scientific report recited on the soundtrack of *Stereo* (1969), or the Kafka-meets-Borges narration of *Crimes of the Future* (1970), and this is appropriate, as *Shivers* is Cronenberg's entrance into the commercial marketplace.[4]

The exteriors and interiors of Starliner Tower are played by Tourelle-Sur-Rive on Nuns' Island, a late work of the Bauhaus architect Ludwig Mies van der Rohe. The structure of the building will provide a physical framework for Cronenberg's choices in this film. The *mise-en-scène* and production design works with the shapes of the rooms made available to the production by their residents, and their existing décor, which the production had little budget to re-dress. This unity of location makes *Shivers*, after *Stereo* and *Crimes of the Future*, the last of three major Cronenberg films to begin, or double, as explorations of a built environment. Cronenberg's imaginary tower-block not only shares its interiors with its real-life double, but also its location; like Tourelle-Sur-Rive, it is situated on an island in the St. Lawrence River, close to Montreal. Apart from naming 'Starliner Island' after its tower, and covering it with a private park in doctored aerial photographs, Cronenberg lightly fictionalises the locale by renaming Champlain Bridge 'Carrier Bridge', a bilingual medical pun. This near-documentary referentiality establishes a naturalistic context for the coming horrors, but it has another significance, beyond the dramaturgy, which is hinted at by the narration we're hearing.

That Merrick's voice speaks in English of a location near Montreal points to the film's plural identity as a Quebecois production made with English-Canadian state financing. English Canada and French Canada had always maintained distinct film cultures. While Quebec had a long tradition of popular genre filmmaking before the brief critical vogue of Direct Cinema documentaries in the sixties, English-Canadian cinema, during the thirties mostly an imperial subsidiary of British 'quota quickie' production, had been stunted since the Second World War by the influence of John Grierson and his anti-artistic model of documentary-making. Although itself blighted by notions of realism during the sixties, Quebecois cinema had entered an expressive recovery towards the end of the decade. With *Valerie* (1969) and *L'Initiation* (1970), director Denis Héroux and producers John Dunning and André Link had inaugurated the wave jokingly known as 'maple syrup porno'.[5] Cronenberg has noted the serious significance of this breakthrough into eroticism for Quebec's predominantly rural, Catholic culture.[6] The films of this cycle remain compelling, explosions of libidinous energy more cinematically expressive, and more revolutionary in their feelings, than the culturally-approved exercises in social realism that surrounded them. It was Dunning and Link who Cronenberg approached as he sought to move from experimental filmmaking to commercial filmmaking, or from the cathedral to the garage. Putting documentary elements at the start of his first commercial feature with their backing,

Cronenberg declares the right of a Canadian filmmaker to the imagination, and reunites documentary with surrealism, its better half since Louis Feuillade conjoined them.

Modernist architecture in cold light, explored by a surrealist imagination, suggests the adjective 'Ballardian'. J. G. Ballard's 1975 novel *High-Rise* was published a few months after *Shivers*' release. Both works concern self-contained luxury buildings whose residents descend into primal behaviour; Ben Wheatley alluded to their similarities when he began his 2015 film of *High-Rise* with a homage to *Shivers*' opening sequence. While a detailed analysis of Ballard's novel in relation to Cronenberg's film is beyond the scope of this book, we can note in passing that a comparison of *Shivers* and *High-Rise* highlights the difference between their authors' sensibilities. Where Cronenberg's threats are biological, Ballard's are psychological; Cronenberg has more faith in the evolution of human consciousness – or, if you prefer, less faith in the irreducibility of human nature. In *Shivers*, the bestial must be *reintroduced*, by a scientific intervention; in *High-Rise*, it only needs to be *awoken*, from a latent state.

The music playing over Merrick's presentation is 'Rooms in a Museum' by Eugene Cines, a library music relative of Satie's *Gymnopédies*. The tone of this piece, initially tranquil, has passed through melancholy into ominousness. As a score, producer Ivan Reitman and Cronenberg's selection is in line with the preference for art music styles since demonstrated in Cronenberg's long collaboration with Howard Shore. Unlike the music heard on other Dunning and Link productions, or Reitman's own *Cannibal Girls* (1974), none of the pieces has a backbeat. The only use of popular music of any sort is diegetic, a drifting guitar instrumental interrupted by the atonal synthesizer squall that introduces a radio newsflash. Most of the pieces heard in *Shivers* sound as if they were already old in 1975, evoking the sonics of previous decades' B-movies. Composed for small ensembles, the cues' stark quality is accentuated by their repeated use; Cimes' piece begins again twice during the film, and like other cues, it's cut off abruptly as soon as the need for music has passed. The music's nature as pre-existing recordings – as *material* – is foregrounded. Thus Cronenberg claims an authorless tradition of vulgar modernity as part of his authored modernist practice. The director knew he was inventing a new kind of horror; he has recalled the uncertainty of his producers about whether or not *Shivers* *was* a horror film[7] – they associated the genre exclusively with the Gothic aesthetics of the Roger Corman Poe films they distributed. In surrounding his new forms with old ones, he meets his sponsors halfway. For the twenty-first-century viewer, another kind of *frisson* is present; heard in the context of hauntology, the stock cues blanket the diegesis with a non-diegetic mist of metatextual ghosts no less apparent to those who haven't heard any of the selections before. Library music is richest when it *sounds* pre-used; only library music could seem to be the soundtrack of Merrick's presentation and the soundtrack of this film at the same time.

Cronenberg places his own writer-director credit over the shot of the building's clinic, the last photograph of the presentation. With a dynamic sense of lift-off, we move from stills to motion, entering the body of the film with a handheld shot, looking up at the tower from a moving car. The car's side window, framing the tower, creates a partial frame within a frame. As the car turns the corner of the road approaching the building, the camera turns to frame the car's occupants, and Merrick's narration concludes.

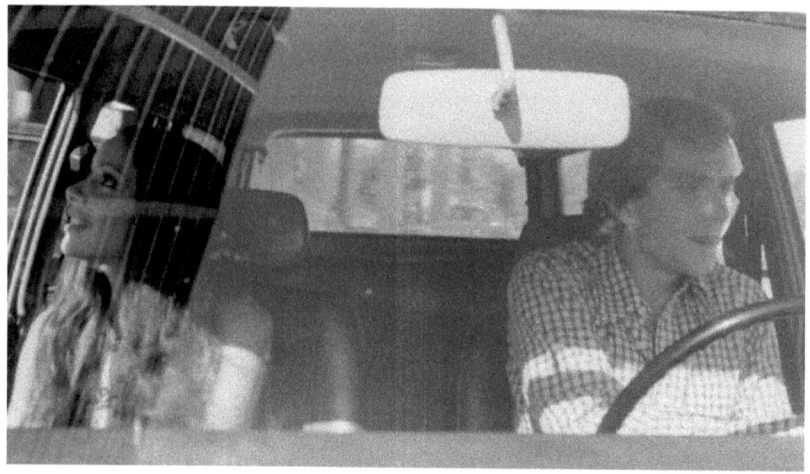

2 – *The young couple*

This affectionate young couple, Kresimer and Benda Sviben (Vlasta Vrana and Silvie Debois) are a way to inject us into the building's bloodstream. Cronenberg introduces them and establishes their characters with one last burst of the silent film acting seen in his first two features, playing their body language without audible dialogue as they walk from the car to the building. In the lobby, we see that the woman is pregnant, a condition soon to be metaphorically echoed both by other residents' bodies and by the building itself.[8] The doorman (Wally Martin) calling the letting agent for them will become more significant. Eager to please and awkward, talking to himself as he finds the right button on his desk, he's working-class light relief of a kind which had ceased to be common by 1975, but which had been a staple of British cinema in the first half of the twentieth century. This becomes clearer in later scenes, and is worth remarking upon in view of the film's reputation as a satirical assault on the middle classes.

As they wait, the woman smiles to the man. Of the twenty-nine shots seen so far (not including black leader), twenty-two have featured glass, and those without it have featured water, chrome or cellophane. Nothing has been opaque yet; everything has been shiny, on display and for sale. Most shots have had subjects far enough from the camera to draw our eyes into the depths of their spaces; the geometry of the general store, dentist and clinic, the building in long shot, the couple behind the reflections in the car's windscreen, and now in the lobby, the glass walls around the three figures, and reflected in the doorman's glasses. One shot briefly foreshadowed the two-dimensional shock to come – the moment where the man, leaving the car, was framed against the building, the glass of the car door, his face and body, and the bright windows of the building appreciable as compiled angles or layers, the depth of the space briefly seeming to contract, but this was a fleeting moment, and still contained reflections, transparencies and striking geometry. The next shot is not only a narrative jolt, but a graphic one.

The next scene introduces us to two characters whose identities we don't find out until they're both dead. In view of Cronenberg's emphasis on the physicality of identity, and to do justice to the density of implication and disorientation in what follows, I'll break with standard practice and leave these figures anonymous until the film identifies them.

An androgynous young woman (Cathy Graham) in a school uniform is standing with her back to a door, which someone is attempting to force open. Against the door in white-walled shallow space, she's exposed, the cold, bright lighting designed to simulate winter daylight in four-walled rooms not designed for filming. Most of the interiors in the film will look like this. Light is being thrown at white or near-white walls to eliminate shadows rather than sculpt them, and our eyes cling to spots of organic texture wherever they appear – as viewers, we are, in a sense, climbing the walls. The perpetual glare of these walls creates a low-level discomfort throughout the film which we don't consciously associate with its visual source. When the parasites appear, part of the comic quality their appearances initially posses stem from the feeling of visual relief we're given by the introduction of organic shapes and textures into these spaces. It would be imprecise to call the effect 'clinical'; the spaces, being real locations, show the awkwardness of their illumination and, as the film progresses, are too fruitfully contaminated by arbitrary physical details to ever seem sterile.

The young woman looks detached from the situation, as though she were listening to the beating on the door more than feeling it against her back. The inwardness of her expression draws our attention to her fresh-faced complexion. What age are we meant to think she is? When the door flies open and she's thrown onto the bed, the row of cuddly toys behind her may be enough to confirm that we are about to witness some kind of attack on a child. Is her underreaction a sign of trauma? The man walking towards her looks concerned rather than aroused. An inappropriate therapist or an abusive parent?

The doorman's assurance that his gun is 'just an advertising gimmick' heightens our unease when Cronenberg abruptly cuts back to the woman and the man struggling on the bed, the juxtaposition seeming to imply that a gun might become necessary. Despite its venue, the struggle's sexlessness continues, as the man keeps everything but his hands as far away from the woman's body as possible; her silence adds to the impression that whatever's happening here is closer to *The Miracle Worker* (1962) than *A Clockwork Orange* (1971). The increasingly kinetic cutting of these last two scenes (twelve shots in twenty-six seconds, including point-of-view shots taking us inside the struggle) is frustrated by a withdrawal to long shot distance and slower action – comically pointed up by the slow progress of Mr. and Mrs. Guilbault (Camil Ducharme and Hanka Posnanska), an elderly French-Canadian couple whose journey across the lobby provides a focus for the camera's pan to frame the entrance of Ronald Merrick.

Ronald Mlodzik had been the lead in Cronenberg's first two experimental features, but this is his only substantial role in the sync-sound narratives. His performance style covers a range from camp mischief to sinister benevolence, which combined with his physical equipment – leading-man height coupled with a head and jaw of substantial sculptural interest – meant he could only ever have been accommodated to commercial film by character casting. His nearest equivalent in Cronenberg's later films is Robert A. Silverman, whose characterisations have a more abrasive, brittle quality. The camera tracks smoothly forward to showcase Mlodzik, who makes Merrick's disengagement and weak levity indefinably sinister. The pan and track through a transparent, reflective space in order to encounter an opaque personality is a scale model of the journey that brought the young couple to this building. His awkward joke ('I assume we're not talking about bachelors, eh?') restates the idea of androgyny. Cronenberg's division of Merrick into seductive voice and carnivorous grin effectively gives Mlodzik a double role, the on-screen one resonating in the context created by the struggle to which we are about to return.

With the cut back to the apartment, the sound of a synthesised heartbeat appears on the soundtrack. The desperation of the struggle increases, the man now plainly terrified. As the woman dives into the frame and onto a couch, her unbroken silence becomes distinguishable from mere speechlessness. She looks back across to the man with an expression which is not quite non-reaction, but a smoothly recovered neutrality, like that of Chantal Akerman's contemporaneous Jeanne Dielman. (It's perhaps only at this point that we perceive how subtle Graham's brief performance is.) As the man bears down on her, she plucks at his arm affectionately. He draws back slightly, and we discover his goal, and the source of his fear, as he begins to strangle her. The significance of his act is suggested by the erotic choreography of the woman's dying moments. The actors' legs are laced together during this action, framing Graham's body for the viewer. As the man drives the woman's throat into the couch, Graham raises and shifts her pelvis, partially exposing her loins as she brings her left leg against Doederlein's right.

Concerning this staging, William Beard has written that 'these elements exist for the heterosexual male viewer's 'pleasure',[9] but, putting aside the heteronormativity of this statement, understanding Cronenberg, and looking seriously at an exploitation film as a work of art, requires all of us, whatever our genders or sexualities, to remove the quotation marks from our pleasure. As expressed in *Shivers*, Cronenberg's materialist intelligence is indivisible from his self-implicating engagement with, and inclusion in, the spectatorship of exploitation film audiences; if we are to understand his intentions or match the acuity of those first audiences, we must implicate ourselves comparably, enrich our enjoyment rather than overwrite or disavow it. We are the audience; how many kinds of pleasure do we enjoy?

The sadism of this scene is relatively soft. The mechanics of strangulation are neither fetishised nor especially realistic – there are no black leather gloves, nor any protrusion of the woman's eyes or tongue. In close-up, we may notice that Doederlein's hands are not meeting around Graham's throat, the left resting where her neck joins her back, and Cronenberg keeps the potentially kinky detail of the school tie's role in her strangulation unemphasised and choreographically vague. The director's priorities are most obvious on the soundtrack; the woman's post-synchronised gasps are unnaturalistically full-throated, , but equally unnaturalistically overwhelmed in the sound mix by the tinnier timbres of the rustling couch and the man's heavy nasal breathing. In short, the site of the act itself isn't the locus of the scene's eroticism; the concepts, their performance and the bodies of the performers are the sources of its *frisson*. While Graham's body is foregrounded, Doederlein's trembling, mask-like grimace, exposing his lower teeth, provides comic distance for viewers who want it, in the first of the film's startling juxtapositions of young and old flesh.

A brief expository scene back in Merrick's office separates the killing from its aftermath. The moment of death itself, which for a conventionally fetishised murder scene would be the 'money shot', takes place off-screen during this action. In long shot behind his desk, surrounded by sunlight and blandly charming after what we've just seen, Merrick's creepy edge seems to have been neutralised.

Our first sight of the dead body is a lyrical image, Graham lying framed on the brown couch cushion against the blue carpet, as though on a life raft, a breeze blowing through her hair. The man's bandage is scientific, using it to silence a corpse is surreal. Smashing a glass of milk with the body's head, he primes the table's surface with a sensual, creaturely layer, evoking both baptism and pregnancy. As he begins to strip the body, Graham gives us the film's first (partial) female nudity.

There follows an exterior tilt, pan and zoom down from one window to another several stories down, an interstitial shot to connect the building's cellular dramatic spaces. The grammatical function of this shot can be paraphrased as '*that* happened *there*, what's next happens *here*'. What makes it worth remarking upon is the inclusion of a superfluous creative decision: the pan left and zoom to a specific window. Neither of the people we're about to meet are visible through the window, later shots appear to place their apartment in a different part of the building, and the apartments' precise spatial relationship never becomes important in any case, so a simple tilt down the building would achieved as much in narrative terms. By making this creative choice for its own sake, Cronenberg turns his first prosaic shot into an existential act: free to direct, he directs.

Our first visit to the apartment of Nick (Alan Migicovsky) and Janine Tudor (Susan Petrie) soon introduces a further location: Nick's body. The convulsions he experiences while brushing his teeth are our first sighting of parasite activity; Migicovsky's physical performance embodies the fantastical situation with total credibility, while the acoustic intrusion of his amplified gasps, laid over the regular whirr of the electric toothbrush, stresses the bodily intrusion. Although this assault is less conventional than the murder, its lack of psychology makes it less mysterious; for the moment, the action we need to understand is physical.

The Tudors are the only residents we spend much time with unaccompanied by our investigator protagonists. Unlike the other significant residents, who are all legibly immigrants to this lifestyle in age or national origin, Nick and Janine come with no specific associations external to Starliner Tower. Respectively queasy/cold and anxious/frustrated, they cover the range of then-conventional fears that high-rise living would produce an alienated, denatured consciousness, and the film's reputation as a satire is probably partly due to their being taken as representative of a type. Nick conducting an extramarital affair with a woman who lives three floors up in the same building is an absurdly keen adaptation to the Starliner dream of hermetically-sealed life, and indicates the building's expansion of social distance; a comparable arrangement in the suburbs would be untenable, like something from the kind of soap opera we'll later hear coming from the Tudors' television.

We return to the murder flat with an insert close-up of the man's hands opening a scalpel. Beneath his hands, the bagful of medical supplies favoured by the composition gives us a burst of the graphic unruliness which will later be contributed by organic objects. The next shot reveals the man shirtless in a surgical mask, an escalation of the assault's surreal fusion of science and brutality. Frontal low-angle framing centres the man, standing behind the table like a priest at an altar. Within this composition, the extremity of the action makes the presence of Graham's underwear incongruous. The conceivable diegetic explanations for why an operation on the woman's stomach would require the apparent removal of all her clothes *except* her knickers are destabilised by

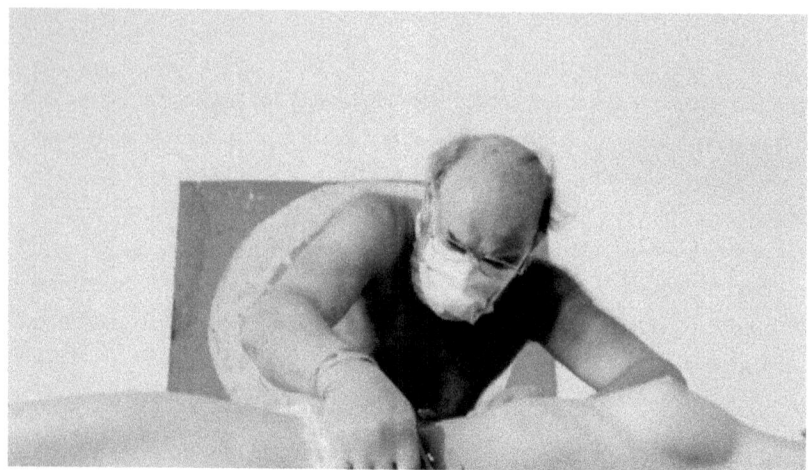

3 – *Autopsy as sacrifice*

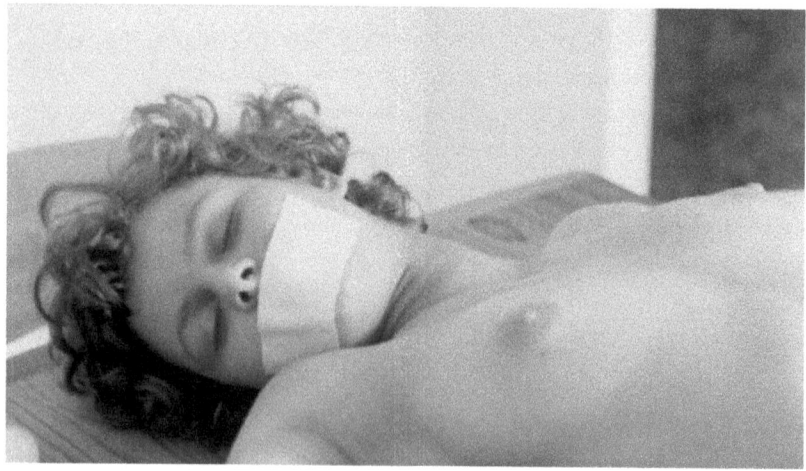

4 – *The repeated close-up*

the combination of possible non-diegetic reasons for the knickers' retention that come to the viewer's mind. Whatever percentage of actor comfort to censorship concerns was involved, the detail can be integrated into the diegesis as a hint of affection, the man preserving the body's modesty, an idea which increases the horror of the tableau.

Staged against a wall hanging of an organically asymmetrical but non-representational shape resembling an eyeball, a sun, a target and a fertilized egg, the pseudo-medical operation on the woman's body has the appearance of a ritual sacrifice. Cronenberg has stated that he believes, contrary to Jung, that 'there are only coincidences',[10] but remembering that he has also called his project 'visionary', and that, in a few minutes, we'll see a quotation from William Blake taped to a shelf in the man's office, it seems relevant to note that Sol is associated in the western esoteric tradition with health, happiness, success – and the temptations of hubris. If the production found this piece at the location, it's a perfect Jungian synchronicity.[11] As an example of modernity's hunger for the newly-eradicable irregularity of organic shapes, it provides a graphic correlative, as we'll later learn, of its diegetic owner's thwarted dream of inoculating modern life against sterility with a dose of the primitive.

When we return to the Tudors, the ugly dull metal of the shutter has become a boundary of cold white light between them. The moist-eyed, devoted expression Petrie gives Janine cools into a closed bitterness in response to his brusque indifference, and even before it does, we can't imagine how Nick ever earned it. The intensity of her masochism as the film proceeds is never met with a comparable depiction of sadism by Migicovsky. Nick's monotonous anger makes Janine's distress seem like an aspirant submissive's expression of frustration with a dominant's inadequate role-playing; he's never cruel in the right way, or at the right time, to provide a stimulus equal to her depth of feeling.

In the murder flat, the man cuts his own throat, and is heard crying out and collapsing over the same medium close-up of the woman we saw during the operation. His suicide takes place in the smallest possible physical space, without disrupting his surreal image – he dies without removing his surgical mask. By restricting the man's collapse to the soundtrack, Cronenberg protects the impact of the frontal composition from diluted repetition. Quebec's two previous horror films involving high-rise apartment blocks had both used them as the venues for suicidal leaps by the victims of devil-worshippers.[12] In both cases, the emphasis was on the buildings' exteriors as symbols of secular modernity, whereas Cronenberg is interested in the interiors of both building and residents, and the material specificities of the location.

When Nick enters the lift, Merrick's suspicious glances give us a picture of what a conformist, hive-like community Starliner must be in its natural state: a man dressed for work but not heading for the garage is a distracting eccentric. Nick's mild exercise of freedom is disrupting Merrick's work, contaminating the three-dimensional brochure experience he's trying to give the young couple with organic human behaviour. Of course, Nick is a suspicious character, but if Merrick already knows that, he shouldn't; the question of how much he knows, and when he knows it, will later become an ominous one, and feeds into our view of his behaviour in this scene on repeat viewing.

Nick's discovery of Annabelle's body triggers another of the convulsions he experienced in front of the bathroom mirror; the parasite appears to be reacting to information relayed to it by Nick's awareness. His exit is marked by a rack focus to the leg in the foreground, a conspicuous technique made more so by it being used not to press her death upon our attention, but as a concluding flourish. Touches of this kind appear as stylistic punctuation throughout the film, but for the most part, Cronenberg's preference for a classical shooting style is already apparent in *Shivers*. Zooms are absent, as they would be from all his work; handheld shots are steady and practical rather than rhetorical, and tripodded shots predominate. Camera movements are motivated by the actions of their subjects, and the subject of a shot is never in doubt. This classicism is also evident on the soundtrack; having decided to enter the horror genre, Cronenberg embraced its narrative mechanisms, and the proportions of his dialogue are closer to those of the classic B-movie than to the loose, oblique, uncommunicative qualities then in vogue. Characters are given speeches, rather than lines, questions are answered rather than left hanging, and action serves exposition. In the 1970s, Canadian and Hollywood filmmakers of all genres had been influenced by the dramaturgy of European modernist film to create ambiguities that were often unsuited to the material they were working on; Cronenberg's understanding of modernism, and of ambiguity, has nothing to do with such obfuscation.

5 – Barbara Steele as Betts – a link to the irrational

Barbara Steele is iconographically overqualified for the role of Betts, and the character's part in the film's narrative and psychic exposition draws much of its power and meaning from this overqualification. The Italian Gothic horror films in which Steele starred during the first phase of her career typically featured her playing a double role, but drew on only half of her equipment – the voice we hear is rarely hers, and always disembodied by the Italian cinema's routine use of post-synchronisation. Stardom is often bound up with material conditions – 'Marlene Dietrich' was Marlene Dietrich-plus-the-right-lighting, 'Louise Brooks' was Louise Brooks-plus-the-right-hairstyle – and after Mario Bava's *La maschera del demonio* (1960) made her an international horror star, the idea that 'Barbara Steele' was Barbara Steele-plus-disembodied-voice followed her as she took roles in English-speaking productions. In *The Pit and the Pendulum* (Roger Corman, 1961), she appears first silent in flashback and then conspicuously dubbed with an American voice, while in *The Curse of the Crimson Altar* (Vernon Sewell, 1968), her own voice is disembodied with an echo effect. (In the latter, Steele's role, her last for six years, is a telling illustration of British cinema's inability to find a place for her qualities – as the witch driving the plot, she's painted green and kept in a zone of ambiguous corporeality, separate from the rest of the film's action.)

Cronenberg met Steele while she was working on *Caged Heat* (Jonathan Demme,

1974) the film with which she returned to acting. In *Caged Heat*, Steele plays McQueen, the sadistic superintendent of a women's prison. Demme sought to make a populist feminist comedy within the women-in-prison genre, and Steele plays McQueen with the appropriate pantomimic breadth. Despite Demme's copious use of post-synchronisation due to acoustic issues with the film's interior locations, Steele's own voice is mostly heard in direct sound. Yet McQueen is a weak character, her sadism more furtive than vital; Steele isn't present for the film's scenes of torture, which are played straight, and her hairstyle and wardrobe conform to the 'repressed spinster' stereotype, with only a dream sequence allowing her usual glamour. In *Piranha* (Joe Dante, 1978), she again speaks freely, even getting the last word, but as with *Caged Heat*, the film is largely comedic, and Steele is not a source of fear *per se*. In *The Silent Scream* (Denny Harris, 1979), the last horror film in this phase of her career, her character is frightening, but child-like and mute. Cronenberg, then, is the only director of Steele's second period to cast her in a role that both engages with her star persona and calls on all her equipment as an actor, while using her to frighten us.

In this first scene, Cronenberg directs Steele to an offbeat, broken-up line delivery, as though she had just read the words through for the first time, drawing our attention to the rhythm and timbre of her voice, as well as the acoustics captured by the direct sound recording. The return of Steele's voice to her image, and to its own physical particularity, coming from within her body in the filmed space, marries with the sense of unemphatic presence created by her use of an understated acting style. Compared to the kind of performance we expect of her, she seems almost not to be acting at all – not just dialling down her persona, but underplaying to a challenging degree. Most of the performances in *Shivers* indicate that Cronenberg, new to directing dialogue scenes, thought it better to err in the direction of too little rather than too much, but in the case of Lynn Lowry, the other actor with whose prior work we're likely to be familiar, this doesn't take her far away from her accustomed strategies.

At present, Betts is simply Janine's indignant friend giving her good advice, and Steele is being her as simply as possible, but casting becomes characterisation: Steele's star persona and history insist that Betts must be doing something to serve her own purposes. We may already wonder whether she's planning a seduction, which will indeed turn out to be the case, although for the time being, our only basis for thinking it is that she's Barbara Steele. An actor's material presence completes what the writing begins; one reason why Cronenberg, always thinking in materialist terms, never storyboards shots, and the difference an actor makes is most obvious when, as in this case, the actor is a star. The expectations Steele's casting creates can also change the film in people's memories; Michael O'Pray's discussion of the film, written at a time when critics were used to having to trust their memories, assigns Lynn Lowry's central role in the conclusion to Steele instead.[13] This is a significant distortion; as we'll see later, the fact that Steele *doesn't* occupy this role is of critical importance to what the film is saying.

When we see Steele acting normally, we are always, as horror viewers, waiting for the other shoe to drop, and in *Shivers*, how it does relates to what the film is saying. Once again Steele plays a double role, Betts before and after infection, with the infection effectively taking the role played by spirit possession in her earlier films. More generally, Barbara Steele is the film's link to all the elements that Cronenberg's version of the horror film ostensibly excludes: curses, vampirism, witchcraft and the inexplicable. So far, *Shivers* follows the investigation of a single anomalous outbreak of irrationality; we have yet to return to the implication of a collective mind in the simultaneity of Nick's wincing and Annabelle's autopsy. In Cronenberg's world of pseudo-scientific modernity, Steele is the horror genre in exile, preserving archetypes and folk memories in a time and place which requires different explanations; she's a refugee or immigrant, like a character in a Val Lewton film. Her casting makes Betts seem as poignant an example of deracination as Mr. and Mrs. Guilbault, the elderly French-Canadian couple we'll meet again later. Steele's Italian pronunciation of 'bravo' in this conversation triggers a world of associations for the viewer – a world of curving drives, ivy-covered walls, great halls, misty lakes and chiaroscuro crypts, now condensed into the tiny space of a luxury flat just outside Montreal. We expect this apartment to be a demonic equivalent of the 'thin places' of Celtic mysticism, where heaven feels closest to earth, and later our expectation will be fulfilled in the material, literal terms of Cronenberg's own world, where even language is physical.

Tudor flees through a basement space large enough to permit a frontal long shot with the back wall of the room parallel to the plane of the screen. The duration of the action gives us time to enjoy an arrangement in white, black, grey and gold, rich in nested rectangles (the breezeblocks forming the wall, the wall itself, the walls visible beyond the door), and offset by the flowing, colourful costumes of the woman and little girl waiting for the lift.

The resemblance between Cronenberg's formalist style and that of Robert Bresson, more generally recognised in films made later in his career, is already discernible in *Shivers* during many of the scenes involving cars. The materialist texture of the sounds of Nick's car door opening and closing here, and the sound, framing and cutting of the later scenes set in this garage, can be cross-referenced to Walter Hill's explicitly Bressonian *The Driver* (1978) a few years later. The next two cuts, which take us to Nick already driving away, and then to him walking through the outer office at work, tighten the linearity that was loosened as our eyes played over the basement shot, and in themselves express pleasure in the options available to sync-sound illusionist narrative filmmaking. By the time Nick gets to work, he appears to be in a trance. Reacting to a murder by going into work as if nothing had happened, he exemplifies one of the forms of bad faith identified by Jean-Paul Sartre: pretending, in Betty Cannon's phrase, 'to be free in a world without facts'.[14] This illusory freedom is evoked by the rapid track-and-pan, atypical of this film's style, with which Cronenberg accompanies Nick's walk to his office.

From the first time we see Roger St. Luc (Paul Hampton), we're detached from his point of view. His arrival at the murder flat and discovery of the bodies, a moment which would have provided the perfect opportunity to attach our perspective to his through shot reverse shot editing, has happened off-screen; we are already on a course running parallel to his awareness rather than identified with it. He's introduced to us via Merrick's answer to the superintendent, and standing out of everyone's way at the far side of the room, an onlooker seen by onlookers. The theme of witness shapes this scene. The room is cut together from a series of shot/reverse shot exchanges: Merrick looking at the superintendent while answering his questions; both looking over at the removal of the woman's body, and seeing St. Luc; Merrick looking up and across at the doctor and the superintendent during St. Luc's brief interview. In the superintendent's affability we're given an indication that, despite this film's originally having been released as *The Parasite Murders*, the criminal investigation is not going to be of primary importance; indeed, after this scene it disappears from the film – no-one ever reports back to him, or suggests that they ought to get in touch with him; the investigator we'll be following is St. Luc. The report of the murder to the police is part of the fabric of reality Cronenberg has to include, a given, and he plays it straight; the superintendent doesn't seem like a detective from a crime film, he seems like a good-natured government employee dealing with members of the public. Cronenberg permits himself one caricatural touch: the avid expression of the police photographer provides the scene with a fleeting subversive note, though of course the photographer is one of us; this is no social criticism, just a cynical chuckle at our shared morbidity.

Now we learn who the killer and his victim were. Hobbes's name has been made much of by some writers, but its irony is relatively basic. *Shivers*' Hobbes, in polar opposition to his seventeenth-century namesake, is a thinker to whom less, not more order seems desirable – but we don't know this yet.

6 – *Comic juxtaposition*

The next scene's opening juxtaposition of jarred specimens with a voice apologising for the lunch provides the speaker and his theme with a comic introduction. The sudden richness of the production design, full of organic clutter, is matched by an abrupt increase in the speed and conceptual density of the dialogue as we meet Rollo Linsky (Joe Silver). Like Hobbes, Linsky shares his name with a philosopher, in this case a then-living one, the analytic philosopher Leonard Linsky. It may be the scientific rigour of analytic philosophy that has dissuaded previous writers from thinking this worth mentioning – it's more difficult to see a good joke in it – but its painstaking formal logic and empiricism, and the real Linsky's specialisation in the philosophy of language, are discursive opposites of his fictional namesake's high-speed, brass-tacks colloquial speech and pragmatism.

The theme of Linsky's dialogue is the visceral identification of food and body. This receives its most direct reference in his line 'to you, organ transplant is just yesterday's kishkas' – a *kishka* being a kind of sausage whose name means 'gut'. 'Guts' in English, as a figure of speech for vitality, will become associated with the physical 'guts' of patients again later in the film, when Linsky discovers the parasite's role in Hobbes' secret project to 'help the guts along'. Hobbes, who had apparently been consumed by the system, will be discovered to have consumed its resources for his own ends. The grotesque equation of consumed and consumer was part of the project he was working on with Hobbes: a parasite which eats diseased flesh and is subsumed into healthy body functioning. Nick's stomach trouble gives us reason to suspect that this 'crazy' idea both worked and didn't work. Between the dialogue and the bodies of its speakers, the superimposition of eater and eaten continues; we think of the 'strong stomach' associated with medical humour as we hear these subjects being brought up light-heartedly during the consumption of food. With the introduction of money, we learn that this room has been fed, or swallowed, by a larger body. The scheme Linsky describes isn't illegal, but he describes it as though it was. As far as he knows, he's been engaged in a semi-disingenuous caper, funded by 'the Northern Hemisphere Organ Transplant Society' on the outside chance that something could come of it which would disrupt their activities. Whereas the classic mad scientist illustrates the idea that idealism leads to derangement, Hobbes' madness erupted from a history of professional and personal cynicism. Did his cynicism drive him mad, or was his madness the culmination of his cynicism? The secret idealism that Linsky will later discover in Hobbes' notes seems to indicate the latter.

In *Shivers*, as in most of Cronenberg's horror films, the source of the danger is private medicine, 'private' in both the 'commercial' and 'personal' senses; later we discover that Hobbes and Linsky's private (commercial) enterprise was a means to Hobbes' private (personal) end. Linsky's account reveals medical research as a business-to-business market. Had it ever been perfected, the organ-replacing parasite would have become the property of the people it threatened to put out of business, and we can imagine them locking it away like the secret cancer cures and electric cars of conspiracy theories. The authored flesh is flesh upon which the authors' corporate sponsors have a claim from the moment of its origination, an idea which anticipates the twenty-first-century controversy over gene patenting. Cronenberg has never used his work to present a political thesis, but ideology is inescapable, and there is something particularly Canadian about his association of the medical industry with cynicism and madness. 'Northern Hemisphere' fudges the politics a little, but this is medicine beyond state boundaries; crucially, the jurisdiction encompasses the United States. Part of what makes people uneasy about Cronenberg is that his honest acknowledgement of the appeal of irrationality coexists with an equally honest refusal to pretend that it constitutes a higher rationality; his view of health and sanity is no closer to capitalist 'freedom' than it is to revolutionary 'liberation'. While Hobbes and Linsky's Robin Hood activities with the Association's money are morally appealing, the very autonomy that makes them possible results in horrors that overshadow any good they might have achieved, even if only because the horrors are the outcome we can see and hear.

Linsky's outlook, and his recollection of Hobbes as a dull pedant and brilliant scammer, seem out of keeping with the romanticism of the William Blake line we see taped to the shelf behind him: 'The road of excess leads to the palace of wisdom.' For the time being, this appears to be a Godardian textual intrusion by the director, to which an objection on the grounds of diegetic implausibility, as a slogan *these* characters would pin up in their office, would be beside the point. Later we'll learn that its incongruity *is* the point. The delayed arrival of this explanation gives us the opportunity to conflate Hobbes's intention and Cronenberg's, and we can compare their methods; Cronenberg had funded *Stereo* by misusing a government literary grant, and the film we're watching is itself the result of state arts funding being put to use on a brazenly commercial venture. Whether imagining Hobbes and Linsky's success inspired Cronenberg to try the same trick, or he wrote his own plan into their heads, he makes their office the venue for a private, pragmatic statement as well as a public, romantic one.

There's more to this framing of cynicism with idealism than the seeding of a mystery or the author's self-amusement, however. The deeper moral analysis of the film, as expressed through its shifting attitude to the events at Starliner Tower, is established by its treatment of Linsky in his first two scenes. In this scene, his company comes as a relief after what we've witnessed; he's amusing and worldly, his desires are intelligible, and he expresses himself more fluently than the other characters we've met so far. We have every reason to like him.

We return to Mona at her desk, rather than to Nick in his office. This goes along with Nick's self-definition in terms of his professional role, but it also increases the distance from which we've been observing him in relation to others. When Mona answers the phone, we discover that the name of the company Nick works for is 'Ashen and Gaunt'. This verbal joke is closely followed by a formalist one, as the diegetic buzzing sound effect of the intercom is mixed high enough to form dissonant chords with the non-diegetic modernist stock cue. Checking in, Mona finds Nick standing like a mannequin over his desk, a position we see in a shot held long enough to make its unnatural stasis evident. Not reacting to this, she begins telling him about the client on the phone despite his silence. 'Nicholas, it's that man whose Lamborghini caught fire on St. Catherine. He's very angry' - the combination of her teacherly, storytelling tone and the arbitrariness of the event being described creates a comic mental picture we feel a mild pang of regret at not seeing followed up. When Nick took the automotive option of coming here, he chose to be evaluated as an automaton. It's only when he fails as an automaton – when he bleeds – that his distress becomes visible to Mona. Having perceived his incapacity to play his role, she becomes nurturing.

He remains unresponsive as she wipes the blood from his mouth in a startling extreme close-up, the far side of his face already soft, his hair and neck a blur. This moment we're given to register his anguish is the closest we get to him, photographically and emotionally. Is he distressed by his failure to occupy his role, by a delayed registration of what he's seen, or by a recognition of his own predicament? We remember that his emotional reaction to Annabelle's murder was immediately joined by the physical reaction of the parasite, and now the physical appears to have induced the emotional. The cut to a two-shot across his desk breaks continuity, his expression now resolute as he again seeks the illusion of control, telling Mona to call him a cab. After his secretary has left the frame, Nick adds one last gesture to his somnambulistic pantomime of working, moving papers on his desk from one pile to another with open, loose hands.

7 – Anguish of bad faith defeated

FOOTNOTES

1. 'Conversation Three', in Moisés Puente ed., *Conversations with Mies van der Rohe*, (New York: Princeton Architectural Press, 2008), p. 57.
2. Tower, or Towers? While this varies during the film, and many sources render it as the latter, Cronenberg frames the two towers of Tourelle-Sur-Rive to look like one, and Merrick can clearly be heard using the singular; they're 'the Starliner Tower Apartments', so I'll be referring to them by the singular throughout, except when quoting dialogue. Singleness and isolation are important attributes of Cronenberg's fictional building, which we see surrounded by a private park in doctored aerial photographs twice during the credits sequence.
3. Northrop Frye, 'Conclusion to a Literary History of Canada', *The Bush Garden: Essays on the Canadian Imagination* (Toronto: Anansi, 1975), p. 226.
4. As in *Stereo*, Cronenberg is also pastiching a form of cinema which is usually excluded from critical discussion, in this case the tape-and-slides presentation. Whereas the images of *Stereo* are too beautiful to be believable in their diegetic role as the product of an academic department's filmmaking unit, *Shivers*' pastiche is an accurate simulation of corporate para-cinematic production. Cronenberg's cognisance of these areas of filmmaking is not atypical of artists in experimental film, a field itself often overlooked or miscategorised. Arthur Lipsett had made pointed and hilarious use of the dire plenty of routine documentary production with his collage films for the National Film Board of Canada, and in the United States, Bruce

Conner drew an implicit parallel between the marginalities of pornographic, industrial and experimental film with his ground-breaking *A MOVIE* (1958).

5. The humour of this phrase, obviously following the pattern of 'Spaghetti Western', has a revealing implication. The West is an intrinsically American milieu, so to make a Western anywhere else has is obviously eccentric, but sexuality is universal. Why would making porn films in Canada be less natural than making them anywhere else?
6. Chris Rodley (ed.), *Cronenberg on Cronenberg* (London: Faber and Faber, 1996), p. 36.
7. Serge Grunberg (trans. Claudine Paquot), *David Cronenberg: interviews with Serge Grunberg* (London: Plexus, 2005), p. 30.
8. The building-as-body idea is echoed in Cronenberg's observations about the Empire State Building as a star and 'role model' for Andy Warhol in the commentary he recorded for 'Supernova – Stars, Deaths and Disasters 1962-1964', a Warhol exhibition he co-curated in 2006 at The Art Gallery of Ontario in Toronto. Like Warhol, whose first commercially-successful film, *Chelsea Girls* (Andy Warhol 1966), features a diverse collection of eccentric Warhol Superstars playing out different scenarios in rooms of the Chelsea Hotel, Cronenberg became a commercial filmmaker with a film of interiors, using the building they share as a physical pretext for the collection of discrete pathologies anthologised by his sensibility. Being an illusionist filmmaker, Cronenberg offers a narrative, as well as a physical, pretext, in the activity of the parasites – with whom his identification is nonetheless clearly indicated.
9. William Beard, *The Artist as Monster: The Cinema of David Cronenberg* (Toronto: University of Toronto Press, 2006), p. 36.
10. Andrew Fish, 'David Cronenberg on Freud, Jung and *A Dangerous Method*', Iconic Interview, June 10 2012, http://www.iconicinterview.com/2012/06/10/david-cronenberg-on-freud-jung-and-a-dangerous-method/
11. Unfortunately, Jung's current mainstream profile as a guru figure for reactionary pop-psychologists makes it necessary to state that Jung is no more the preserve of the right than Freud is the preserve of the patriarchy. Recognising the shadow enables us to wield its energy in consciousness to progressive ends, as demonstrated in the spiritualities of cultures such as the feminist urban witch movement, who create their own pantheons and rituals, harnessing the potency of the irrational mind to their rational intellection and choice. To leave such a rich source of imagery, myth and poetry to reactionaries would be self-defeating.
12. *Le diable est parmi nous* (Jean Beaudin, 1972) and *The Pyx* (Harvey Hart, 1973).
13. Michael O'Pray, 'Primitive Phantasy in Cronenberg's Films', in Wayne Drew (ed.), *David Cronenberg (BFI Dossier 21)* (London: British Film Institute, 1984), p. 50.
14. Betty Cannon, *Sartre and Psychoanalysis: An Existentialist Challenge to Clinical Metatheory* (Lawrence: University Press of Kansas, 1991), p. 46.

Second Reel

Screen space flattens again with the cut to a black-and-white photograph of Annabelle and a friend on Linsky's office wall. In the ensuing dialogue, it's confirmed that Hobbes' relationship with Annabelle began when she was underage. Having reassured us before, Cronenberg now drops us back into the queasiness of our initial impressions. When Linsky says 'I'll never understand how he could do what he did to her', it may take us a moment to understand that the 'what' he has in mind is only the murder. Having accepted his cynicism, we're put in a disturbing position by the revelation of his deeper amorality. His apparent distaste for Hobbes's relationship with Annabelle didn't preclude his collusion in it, and he apparently raised no objection to Hobbes bringing her to their office. This exposure of our boundaries is what much of *Shivers* is engaged in, but for the twenty-first-century viewer a kind of unease is created by this moment which isn't quite like those evoked by the rest of the film. Being accustomed to explicit condemnation of anyone even tangentially involved with child sexual abuse, we're likely to feel disconcerted by the sense that Cronenberg is leaving us to decide how much to feel about Linsky's involvement.

A taboo must be given its due before its transgression can release energy; in Georges Bataille's description, 'the forbidden action takes on a significance it lacks before fear widens the gap between us and it'.[15] It's the thwarting of this release, more than a moral objection to an attitude such as Linsky's being imagined by his author, that makes this seem like a lapse of attention. The film's later scenes of rape, paedophilia and incest, however blackly comic, all evoke our horror and acknowledge the taboos they transgress; Cronenberg's awareness of the gravity of his visions isn't in doubt. By contrast, Linsky's complacency in this scene presents no obstacle to his later becoming, however ironically, the closest thing the film has to a Van Helsing, and viewers watching the film for the first time today are likely to be at least momentarily distracted by the feeling that it *should*. If we compare Linsky's predicament and death to those of later Cronenberg characters like *The Brood*'s (1979) Hal Raglan or *Scanners*' (1981) Paul Ruth, our queasiness is relieved to an extent; although a stooge rather than a perpetrator, he remains, like them, complicatedly admirable, contemptible and culpable, and dies in a way which, while feeling as senseless as all deaths do in Cronenberg's films, can be taken as a traditional 'atonement' to whatever degree we feel the need to identify one.

Linsky moves to the corner of the room as though seeking the professional security of the laboratory equipment there, the camera panning to follow him as the theme we heard over Merrick's presentation is repeated for the first time. A close-up of St. Luc, abruptly cheerful, saying 'Well...' is inserted into the pan, which is completed in the next shot. The association of a change of subject with a shift in blocking is executed on-screen this time. Linsky and St. Luc's incongruously 'street' parting handshake expresses the desire for another kind of security, a physical sign between characters who are, after all, bereaved friends, though neither they nor the exposition have time for a performance of mourning. The men restore the lightness of their earlier conversation with a flight into triviality; we haven't seen the last of St. Luc's 'used' pickle.

Nick has arrived home. He crosses the lobby in the background of a shot the low angle of which is rationalised by the presence of Garbage Room Man (Wally Martin), a janitor, sitting on the floor in the foreground to work on the doorman's intercom desk. This camera angle showcases the interlocked rectangles of the lobby's glass walls. The buildings seen in Cronenberg's first two experimental features contained many open, amphitheatre-like spaces, constructed on several levels, permitting clear lines of sight for social gathering. This building has no comparable spaces; most of it is divided between corridors and private apartments. This is one of the few Starliner interiors to incorporate a pleasing architectural prospect. Nick's distance from us and proximity to this geometric arrangement suggest his reabsorption into the structure from which we saw him flee. He won't leave the building again. As the camera makes a diagonal tilt to take in Nick's silent, distracted nod in response to his greeting, we see that the doorman is reading a novelette from the 'Hospital Romance' series of the Woman's Weekly Library. The title of this volume is unclear; the one he follows it with will be allotted an identifying insert close-up.

The next shot introduces Nurse Forsythe (Lynn Lowry). In view of what we'll learn about her relationship with St. Luc, it's appropriate that her first appearance is staged so as to draw our attention away from her. Framed at a 45-degree angle, her desk forms a curved triangle, pointing to a beam which bisects the frame. On its right, Janine and Parkins (Al Rochman) are engaged in a one-sided conversation. If we are looking at Forsythe already, it's because we want to look at her – like Parkins, whose attention switches in her direction as she raises her wrist to check her watch, drawing ours if we've been watching for plot.

Prior to *Shivers*, Lynn Lowry had appeared in two other horror films, *I Drink Your Blood* (David Durston, 1970) and *The Crazies* (George A. Romero, 1973), both productions with large casts in which she plays a quiet woman infected by a mind-altering illness, her performances of gentle derangement used as chilling punctuation to stretches of loud, violent behaviour, largely by male characters. Both films attempt topicality; despite radically different degrees of formal sophistication, both feature scenes of self-immolation – not by Lowry's characters – as sledgehammer references to Vietnam.

Both films also suggest that existing conditions have contributed to her current state; in *I Drink Your Blood*, Lowry plays an intellectually disabled (and mute) member of a cult whose Charles Manson-like leader doses his followers with a sacrament of LSD, while Cathy, her character in *The Crazies*, is the daughter of an over-protective widowed father who may have been sexually abusing her before either of them was infected. *I Drink Your Blood* was made while the Manson Family trial was still ongoing. Attending to its cynical business, it reveals fascinating ambivalence about hippies, small towns, Manson and his followers' crimes, but these go unstressed, and the film's rich seams of misogyny, racism and classism suggest that nothing more considered than hypocritical prurience was at work.

Lowry's role in *The Crazies* is more substantial. Her first line – 'I heard you say you were Dr. Brookmyer's nurse? I'm the appendectomy' – would no doubt have appealed to Cronenberg, who decided to cast her after seeing the film, which he otherwise disliked.[16] The difference between Lowry's use by Romero and her use by Cronenberg reflects the directors' different attitudes to ambiguity.

For Romero, ambiguity is a result of militarism and paranoia. The well are mistaken for the sick; the hero fires on friends, mistaking them for enemies. This ambiguity is frightening, but it isn't interesting; the equivalence of ordinary American 'madness' to the behaviour of the 'crazies' is stated, then repeated, though Romero's assertive style ensures that this repetition remains stimulating. The line between sane, liberal-minded Us and insane, intolerant Them is thick and emphasised without irony, and the moments at which characters cross between the two states are always certain; while they may move back and forth between normal and abnormal behaviour, they don't display behaviour which could credibly be both.

Lowry comes closest to breaking this rule. In her scene with Clank (Harold Wayne Jones) in the country club kitchen, Cathy seems like a well-meaning but slightly spaced-out hippy, the logical disconnections in her thinking emphasised by Romero's rapid editing. When Clank pulls away from her touch, Lowry's delivery of Cathy's line, 'I have it don't I? I have the disease' opens up existential possibilities that the film's political analysis has no room to accommodate. If her fear were only a reaction to Clank's, *The Crazies* would be a different kind of film, but we've already seen the evidence of Cathy's infection. As Clank leaves, Cathy takes her hand away from her face and looks from it to her arm with a suspicious, uneasy expression. This reaction locates the infection in her body, not in the mind, as a more conventional gesture of dizziness or head-clearing would. The Cartesian predicament Lowry depicts here, the mind looking with distrust at the body of which it is part, has obvious Cronenbergian resonances. In moments like these, her performance in *The Crazies* indicates the possibility of a sustained portrayal of a liminal state, both threatening and unthreatening, healthy and sick.

Considering Nurse Forsythe in relation to Lowry's previous horror roles gives us only a partial picture, however. She had played significantly larger and more central roles outside the horror genre, in *Sugar Cookies* (Theodore Geshuny, 1973) and *Score* (Radley Metzger, 1974). *Sugar Cookies* was a Mary Woronov vehicle set in the porn industry and itself midway between sexploitation and softcore, while *Score*, widely seen in a softcore version, features male-male hardcore scenes. If we take into account the relative duration and significance of Lowry's roles in these four films, and split the difference between the films' plural genres, it's arguable that at the time of *Shivers*' shooting, Lowry was more a softcore porn star than a horror star. Whether or not it meant anything to Cronenberg, this fact wouldn't have been lost on 'maple syrup porno' pioneers Cinepix. Lowry's recollections that during the making of *Shivers*, she was asked if she'd be willing to do full-frontal nudity (she refused), and that it wasn't clear which film the producers had seen her in[17] indicate that this stream of her work may have done as much to qualify her to play Forsythe as her horror performances did. In both her horror and her erotic films, Lowry's characters are submissive, and in *Sugar Cookies* her dual role makes her a victim twice over. Only in *Score* is she given a character arc to portray that points towards Forsythe's autonomy.

In Score, Lowry plays Betsy, an innocent Catholic wife who, alongside her husband, is initiated by a libertine couple into recreational drug use, bisexuality, kink and group sex in one night. By the next morning, she has become an enthusiastic orgiast, and immediately leads her husband into further adventures. If we play the game suggested by Jean-Luc Godard when he claimed that Jean Seberg's character in his *A Bout de Souffle* (1960) was so related to her role in *Bonjour Tristesse* (Otto Preminger, 1958) as to permit his film to be appended to Preminger's with the titlecard 'three years later',[18] we could view *Shivers* as the further adventures of Betsy – '[Trilby]… bearing a remarkable resemblance to Frankenstein's monster' in the words of Elvira (Claire Wilbur) in Metzger's film, infiltrating deep Catholic territory as a subversive agent of polymorphous perversity. Seen in this context, Forsythe's attempts to rescue St. Luc from sexlessness make *Shivers* a gender-swapped sequel to Cinepix's *Valerie*. An undetected seducer from the first time we see her, Forsythe is the most proactive character Lowry played during the 'seventies.

Cronenberg cross-cuts Nick's return home with Janine's talk with St. Luc about him. Nick enters the apartment in a shot which at first appears handheld, before an upward tilt as it begins a sideways track (incorporating a slight pan) reveals the initial small movements to have been the mild unsteadiness of an operator-held unlocked tripod head, loosened for quick movement. The instability creates a sense of unease, while the tilt serves to preserve Migicovsky's headroom in the frame. As he sits on the couch and reaches for a drink, we notice first the collection of African tribal masks which appeared in the background of the breakfast scene, a sign again of the desire to import 'authenticity', and a sense of unmediated experience. We also notice how much of the Tudors' furniture is (in this light, at least) white or red. Red phone, lampshade, couch frame; white ashtray, ornaments, and a largely white work of art on the wall. Nick's face is almost as white as his shirt and the wall behind him. In a graphic sense, we could say that this is the most Canadian shot in the film.

At the clinic, St. Luc is reassuring. He refers to an indulgent diet that Migicovsky's slender frame belies, which suggests that at some point, Nick's behaviour and interaction with

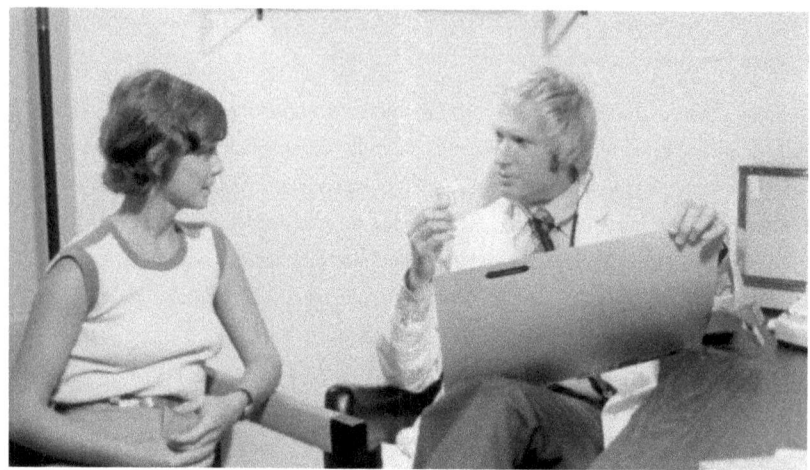

8 – Janine and St. Luc

the parasite was conceived of in terms of the representation of an oral fixation, rather than the masturbation analogy it now appears to be. Hampton and Petrie's performance of St. Luc's interaction with Janine in this scene is his most leading man-like moment; he doesn't really seem the inhibited character we'll later take him for, but more on the slight dissonance between role and performance later. We get a hint from his addressing Forsythe without looking at her, and her expression as she walks away, of the conflict which will later be more fully developed – though by no means conclusively, as we'll see.

In the apartment, Nick collapses; we can add Migicovsky's tongue, which has been painted, to the inventory of red items. The camera's quick tilt down to watch him lying on the floor, followed by a slow track and pan away, adds a suspicion of misanthropy to the unease we felt during his previous shot, and the detachment already in evidence. An ellipsis follows, again creating distance, as he goes to vomit into the bath, and our perspective on him is that of a voyeur. After he's left the bathroom and walked into off-screen space, a cut to a brief shot of the blood in the bath further accentuates the distance between our consciousness and his; we are watching him at both an emotional and a physical remove. The Tudors' apartment appears to have migrated within the building's body; it's now at a corner of the building, with a balcony which Nick now leans over and vomits from. The inclusion of balconies in Tourelle-Sur-Rive's design was uncharacteristic of Mies, just as the breadth of this joke will become of Cronenberg. An artist approaching his end, and another setting out, share their compromises as they pass each other – *what could it hurt now?* meets *what have I got to lose?*

On its first appearance, inching through the grass, the parasite is greenish-brown and covered in blood. Its appearance suggests a sapient stool which has decided to swim salmon-like against Nick's digestive current to emerge from the mouth. The colour and action of the parasites, as variable as the symptoms of the infected, will suggest different analogues in different scenes, each appearance a discrete aesthetic event. The two ladies' line of travel appears to be towards a grass bank; they are walking into 'the distance' conceived of in a stylised, comic-strip way, as though the horizontals beyond them were painted on a cyclorama. This receding into unreal life, without necessity or dynamism, expresses the director's fear with the Beckettian sense of desolate/deadpan comic staging seen in *Transfer* (1966), his first short, in which a psychoanalyst's office is a set of office furniture in the middle of a snow-covered field.

As they walk off, the younger woman's 'Now come along, and we'll get you tucked into bed before the colour TV' is an unfortunate line, seeming like a gratuitous stab of social satire. Should she be hitting the nightclubs instead? If, as he has often stated, Cronenberg's impetus to make horror films had initially come from his recognition of mortality in the ageing process, then this joke expresses a deep fear. As an underground filmmaker in the previous decade, his identity had been bound up with a youth-identified culture; on some level, losing youth meant a loss of identity. If the bourgeois stability of Starliner Tower wasn't appealing to him on some level, it wouldn't be a tomb he could imagine being sealed up in – *Shivers'* fear of Starliner life is a kind of claustrophobia.

At the clinic, Parkins repeats his monologue about slowing the ageing process to another woman. If we hadn't been sure before, we've now classified him as a comic type, an obvious old roué. Forsythe calls Parkins through for his appointment by his first name, Brad, the first name we hear him given. While examining him, St. Luc will call him 'Mr. Parkins' once, but speaking quickly and quietly, he swallows the words. 'Brad' is the name we remember him by, a name which sounds young, and younger for a man of his age in the mid-1970s. As an abbreviation, it implies familiarity, intimacy, friendliness. In the

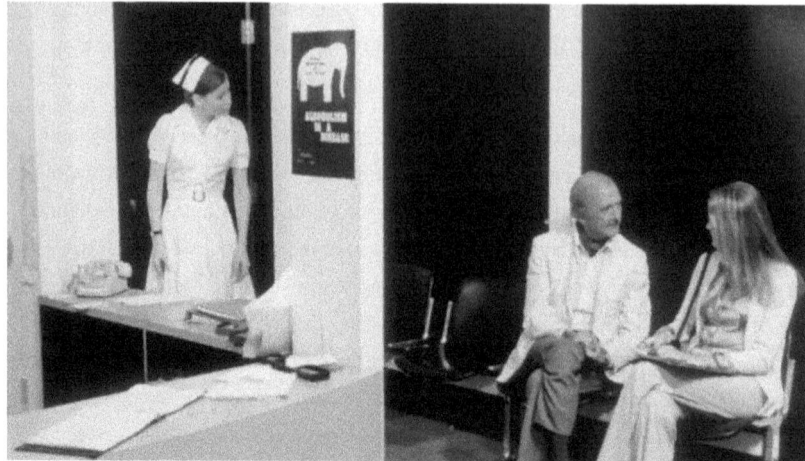

9 – Roué interrupted

end credits he will be 'Parkins' only, weighed down by years in his reduction to a paternal name, while a newsflash tells us of the crimes of the infected.

As we might expect, Brad flirts with Forsythe once he's alone with her, responding to her parting instruction to take his shirt off with 'You don't have to go, I'm not shy.' Surprisingly, she responds with a flirtation of her own: 'Now don't be a tease, Brad! I'm still working, you know.' Lowry delivers the second sentence with a playful cock of her head. Rochman's stilted delivery of Brad's already-flat reply 'Yes, I know' as Lowry leaves the frame is followed by several seconds of Brad alone, removing his shirt. This is a moment of dead time, unless we recognise the exposure of his torso as a disclosure of new information.

A situation familiar from 'saucy' comedy – the *Carry On* series (1958-1978) was big in Canada – has been turned into something unnerving. The reclassification of Brad's libido from stock joke to narrative factor introduces the utopian theme of the film: the reclamation of all flesh as 'erotic flesh'. The comedy of *Shivers* encourages our defensive laughter not merely to share it, but in order to draw our attention to its defensiveness. Within a few seconds, a stock character has been embodied, and the rhythmic oddity of the scene's conclusion seems to build on the flatness of Rochman's line and delivery to switch the focus from characterisation to physicality.

A right-to-left tracking shot begins with the camera already in motion, parallel to the wall. As with the static frontal shot earlier, we're in the basement, and following the journey of a figure who enters from frame right. This character is listed in the credits as Laundry Woman (Nora Johnson). Functional labels like 'Laundry Woman' aren't generally given to identification figures, but in this film every body matters, and Laundry Woman's is especially auspicious, being the parasites' first on-screen target. She's overweight and middle-aged, her eyebrows are carefully plucked if not drawn on, and she's wearing a loud print dress. A greenish high-angle light, its source out of frame, sculpts the right side of her face as she passes it. The light matches the dominant colour in her dress, creating a push-pull of individuation from, and submergence in, her environment. When she leaves the frame, the camera pulls focus, as it did when Nick left the murder flat, to emphasise something we've already noticed: the blood trail leading from the air vent.

This scene's editing proceeds according to the conventional post-*Psycho* structure, building tension with a relatively long take of Johnson's comic performance before exploding into rapid cuts of the parasite's attack. Three point-of-view shots in two seconds abruptly shorten the comic distance – we occupy this endangered body as we occupied the struggling bodies of Hobbes and Annabelle, but without the perspective of the attacking parasite, part of the scene's impact is the shock of identification: the othered body is our own. Cronenberg's sense of human solidarity is rooted in his sense of our shared indignity; this underlying pessimism has sometimes led unwary critics to mistake him for a misanthrope.

The parasite has already changed: meat-red, it now resembles a large leech both sculpturally and behaviourally. Johnson maintains the breadth of her performance during the struggle, which is protracted enough for its mixed register to create discomfort in the viewer; suspending us between horror and the giggles, Cronenberg again turns an easy joke into a source of comic unease. The woman's last groan before we return to the clinic is ambiguous, foreshadowing the behaviour of the infected.

In the clinic, St. Luc's 'How are ya?' to Brad is heard with neither man in the frame – for a second, we're looking at a slightly soft image of installed medical equipment. This time, the awkwardness of Brad's reply is naturalistic rather than wooden. These consulting room scenes appear to have been filmed in a real consulting room, and the naturalism of this scene is enhanced by the room's unhelpful acoustics; every physical movement Rochman and Hampton make is amplified, and a loud background rumble is heard throughout. This real room is giving a bad performance as a fictional one – a useful passing reminder that fidelity to material reality breaks down the illusionist 'transparency' of realism.

The problem being so much worse here than it was in the scene between Brad and Forsythe underlines the difference between the discourse we heard there and this professional encounter, as does Rochman's audible projection of his lines. Hampton's lower volume and underplaying helps Rochman, contextualising his delivery as a characterisation rather than a technical limitation. We'll remember that St. Luc doesn't call Brad 'Brad'. These two scenes plant a suspicion in our minds that something is already going on under the doctor's nose, or perhaps over his head.

10 – Modernist flashback

St. Luc's preoccupied affect resumes in his response to Brad ('Oh yeah? Better than me, my man, better than me'). Brad says that he found Annabelle's lumps 'kind of sexy'. Brad's desire for youth has inspired him with an indiscriminate attraction to anything new, even a new kind of sexually-transmitted infection. This lust-spurred obsession with novelty is, up to a point, a parody of the *Playboy* philosophy. As we'll discover, this appetitive utopianism makes Brad an ideal candidate for the parasite. As he speaks, one of the film's stylistic one-offs occurs, a three-shot flashback on the visual track to remind us where 1511 is and who Annabelle Brown was. The first of these shots has the same composition as the shot Nick entered when he arrived at the flat and opened the door, and is presumably taken from the same take, the second is a long shot of Annabelle braced against the door that we didn't see earlier, and the third is an earlier section of the first shot we saw of her. The cuts' speed, the use of a previously unseen composition, and the shots' silence, accompanied by the ongoing sound from the room to which we now return, all recall the example of the French New Wave, and particularly Alain Resnais, whose influence had then recently been imported into the horror genre by Nicolas Roeg's *Don't Look Now* (1973). Yet whereas Resnais and other film modernists had used such techniques to free their work from the narration-machine standards of classical film form, Cronenberg seems to have inserted this moment to aid expositional clarity. The cinematic thrill it provides inclines us to forgive its redundancy, but it makes us wonder: did Cronenberg think we needed this reminder because the noise around Rochman's voice might distract us from the information Brad is disclosing, or because we're easily distracted? Acknowledging a spectatorship not primarily invested in plot is probably part of the reason, but the highlight it adds to the scene, which would otherwise be a continuous, cramped and badly-recorded take of pure plot carpentry, requires no explanation.

A melancholy flute-led piece begins on the soundtrack, and continues over the following scene. Janine is seen visiting the Starliner's shop. As we've just been reminded, realism requires illusionist labour, and the reality of this tiny interlude is carefully constructed. Janine's magazine is heard being placed on and picked up from the counter in clear foleyed sound, while the shop assistant speaking to the next customer is completely silent; Janine's subjectivity is the focus.

When Janine opens the door into the corridor, a cardboard cut-out man in a display ad for Carlsberg beer appears to look through the doorway, directly into the camera. Judging from its absence from previous analyses of the film, product placement is the most taboo aspect of *Shivers*' *mise-en-scène*. Both Carlsberg and Coca-Cola make prominent appearances in *Shivers*, and are listed among the 'Acknowledgements' in the end credits. Each appearance is prominent and sustained enough to suggest that money changed hands, though what percentage of the film's costs their inclusion covered is something for a scholar with access to the production paperwork to discover. While a specific space-time event like a building, or an actor's body, can become part of a filmmaker's personal world while the film lasts, around brands the register always becomes documentary; every shot of a logo recalls all our other encounters with it. Neither Carlsberg's logo nor Coca-Cola's has changed in the interim, but the willingness of both to place their products in a film with *Shivers*' themes is itself 'period' in its open amorality – in 1974, they were as happy to appear in our nightmares as in our dreams. Today, brands employ people to worry about connotation; cognisant of their corporate personhood, they have to be mindful of the neighbourhoods they're seen in. Considered as people, the Carlsberg and Coca-Cola of 1974 seem to have been 'integrated characters', at ease with the human condition and their relation to it.

After walking up a corridor more shadowy than any we've seen so far at Starliner Tower, with an Exit sign at its far end, Janine walks into Betts' living room without having to be let in, and without us seeing the apartment's front door from either side. The theatrical quality of her entrance is enhanced by the move from shadows to bright artificial light. Together, these two shots reinforce our sense that Betts' apartment is a different kind of space from those lived in by the other Starliner residents. Because it's the most individualistically furnished of the apartments we see in *Shivers*, it's also the one that seem most designed, an impression which, combined with its consistently artificial lighting, makes it seem more of a 'movie' space.

Behind Janine during this exchange, we see evidence of Betts' organic taste: a shelf of bottles, books, a Deutsche Grammaphon LP facing forward like a picture. As in her first scene, Betts' shots show her surrounded by plants; her home is an outpost of cultivation, in both senses. We never see her reading a magazine or watching television, both of which become increasingly loaded activities as the film progresses. As well as creating a different kind of space, Betts also occupies space differently; we first saw her lounging on the bed with Janine, now she's sowing on the floor, cross-legged and barefoot.

The unconvincing enthusiasm with which she greets the information that 'Dr. St. Luc's gonna come and see Nick about ten' is our first indication that, as we expected of a character played by Barbara Steele, Betts has some purpose of her own. Our hopes are confirmed as she invites Janine for dinner. The mismatch between Janine's feelings and those of Betts is accentuated by the fact that this scene is a series of shot/reverse shots of Petrie and Steele, and Cronenberg boldly emphasises the disjunction, his direction of the actors risking our suspicion that neither was in the presence of the other when their half of the scene was shot. Betts' tone of voice is low and seductive, Janine's chirpy and casual. Janine doesn't pick up on Betts' lack of interest in her update, and her acceptance of the invitation with 'Okay!' and a wave, miming 'buh-bye', is a comic under-reaction.

11 – Janine visits Betts

Throughout this scene, the melancholy stock track begun as we left Brad and St. Luc has continued. Because it accompanied Janine alone on her walk to visit Betts, we thought of it as a response to the poignancy of her situation. As we watch Betts pressing the wine glass to her lips, looking at the space Janine just vacated, it seems to have attached itself to Betts' perspective. The piece fades out during the next shot, which begins with Janine halfway into the frame and out of focus, the frame dominated by the steep vertical of corridor wall between her and the next apartment doorway, which the composition turns into a broad white stripe and a thin red one. She comes into focus as she approaches, in an optical expression of the psychic distance between where she's been and where she's going. This red stripe turns out to be the Tudors apartment.

Cronenberg concludes this modernist shot by deploying a classic horror trope: Janine finds the door already open.

Inside the Tudors' apartment, the open fridge is the only source of light, and two Coca-Cola cans make their first prominent appearance. (A single can, its logo not clearly shown, appeared over Linsky's shoulder during the lunch scene.) Bearing the only recognisable logo on any of the items occupying the shot's brightest point, their familiarity dominates the screen during the seven seconds it takes Janine to enter, turn on an off-screen light, close the open front door and call out to Nick. During this dominance, however, something far more significant to the aesthetic pattern of the film is taking place. The tungsten warmth of the light turned on by Janine sculpts her face and body in chiaroscuro, in contrast to the overexposed white haze from the fridge, and this way of lighting Petrie will become of major subtextual importance within the film's formal exposition.

A handheld point-of-view shot shows Nick's hand beneath the fridge door. On repeat viewing, Cronenberg's choice of this moment to show Janine's perspective for the first time stands out like an early clue in a mystery. In a return to the previous set-up, the camera follows Janine in a diagonal tilt downwards, revealing Nick collapsed on the floor, half propped against the fridge. As she cleans his face, just as we remember his secretary doing, a brief closer two shot shows him looking at her with pathetic sullenness. His incapacity, and our awareness of his predicament, changes the dynamic between them. Coaxing him to stand up as though talking to a child, she gets him to his feet and out of the room, turning on the light as she leaves. In a close-up of the door now diegetically illuminated by the kitchen light out of frame, a blood trail to the open letterbox indicates that another parasite has left him; again a blood trail stands in for a more elaborate special effect.

In the corridor, two children, a girl and a younger boy, are shouting through letterboxes. They are unactorly, credibly the children of a real building's residents rather than professional actors, and their performances give this scene a documentary quality. An extreme close-up shows a parasite emerging from a letterbox they haven't reached yet, presumably the Tudors'. On seeing it, the children are as amused by its appearance as disgusted; neither is afraid. The boy approaches to pick it up, the girl holds him back while expressing comic disgust herself. When they run off, they scream, but without real fear. What better defence of the horror genre? The last shot of this interlude shows that the parasite has already moved on.

Cut to Linsky back at the university, opening a can of Coke and drinking. He appears not to have yet eaten the rest of St. Luc's 'used' lunchtime pickle, but presumably this is a different one, at least diegetically. The possibility it raises that the same half-pickle is playing both roles – we picture it being preserved uneaten between camera set-ups – is the only time the production doesn't seem to have exactly as much money as it needs. Apart from establishing that Linsky is working late and doesn't know what's going on, the main function of this shot is the delivery of another slogan, this time a Cronenberg original: 'Sex is the invention of a clever venereal disease.' The attribution of this quotation to Emil Hobbes is partially obscured by Linsky standing before the fridge, making it effectively a Godard-like on-screen text statement from the director himself, with Linsky positioned in order to frame it, like a figure in an illustrated primer. Yet this shot, confrontational to us, must have been reassuring to Coca-Cola – six shots after the Tudors' cans, here is a clarification that you don't have to vomit blood to want Cokes in your fridge.

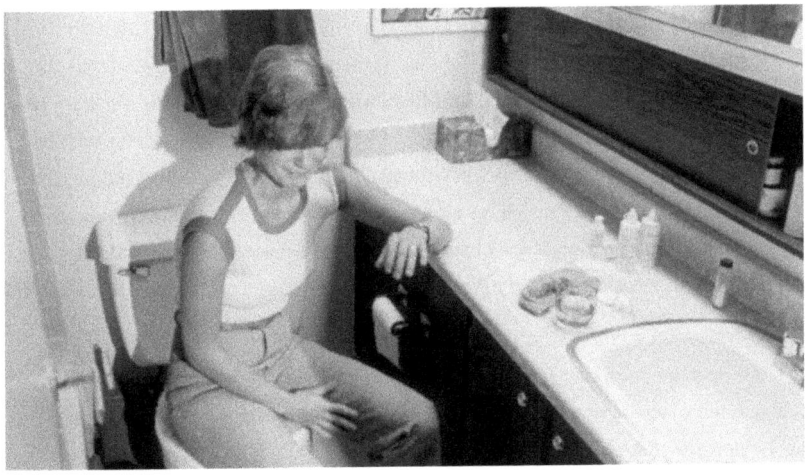

12 – Janine takes a pill

At the Tudors' apartment, Janine enters the bathroom and discovers the blood. In perhaps the film's most telling moment of sociological witness, her reaction is to take a pill, presumably a tranquilliser. In the bedroom, Nick addresses the parasite in his stomach as if it were an animal he was attempting to domesticate ('Come on, boy... you and me are going to be good friends'), an interaction of the anthropomorphising occupied and the anthropomorphised occupier which recalls myths about tapeworm behaviour. This is the most animation we've seen from Nick, indeed the only time we see him expressing enthusiasm about anything, and it's the beginning of the parasites' takeover. As soon as the pulsing in his stomach has restored any revulsion the parasitetakeover. As soon as the pulsing in his stomach has restored any revulsion the parasite may have lost for us after the children's laughter, Cronenberg uses it to resume the comic tone. Addressed anthropomorphically, it responds anthropomorphically; its abrupt 'ducking' when Janine enters in response to Nick's voice is a remarkable technical achievement by Joe Blasco's team – a joke that requires comic timing from non-actors, executed on a film without money for many takes – and immediately analogises the morbid, alien dynamic between Nick and his occupier to a legible comic model: a masturbation joke. Funny as it is, it introduces the parasite's undermining of identity, the key issue of the film. Drawing on Lacan, Manfried Riepe has proposed that the parasite 'acts in the sense of a cancellation of castration: it is the lack of the lack... with the parasite in his stomach, [Nick] is completed by the "reified phallus"'.[19] As far as the masturbation analogy extends, this is true, but Riepe's notion implies self-satisfaction, when the *dissolution* of the self is arguably the real source of Nick's pleasure. His desire to help the parasites is of a piece with his decision to go to work after discovering Annabelle's murder; he has embraced a *raison d'etre* imposed by other forces. Viewed in relation to Cronenberg's metaphoric coupling of architecture and the body, Nick's body is a hive; in this respect, he resembles Starliner Tower more thoroughly than the other infected residents we'll encounter.

Janine enters the scene in silhouette, having entered the room off-screen. For the moment, the mildly ominous aspect this gives her is simply an anomaly. Two unexpectedly large lampshades, representing marine plant fronds in shades of green and light blue, draw the eye, their colours reminding us of Betts' plants. If we remember the 'primitive' wall-hanging in the murder flat, it occurs to us that where a space is shared, Cronenberg is as likely to use production design to support the psychology of the characters with whom it shares the frame as he is to use it to express the psychology of the characters with whom the space has initially been identified. We assume that these lampshades reflect Janine's taste, because her relationship with Betts is more sympathetic than her relationship with Nick, and because we first see them sharing screen space with her. As Janine comes out of the shadow, the lighting reintroduces the contours of her body, and our attention is unavoidably drawn to Petrie's prominent nipples. These appear periodically throughout the film; anticipating the polymorphous perversity to come, the most androgynous dresser of the main female cast has also been the most consistently sexualised by her costume. Janine's tight T-shirt and jeans have been tiding our voyeurism over since Cathy Graham's nudity as Annabelle's body, and her attractiveness increases our sympathy for her. As she sits next to him on the bed, the chain and crucifix around her neck glinting in the light, Nick's silence seems like childish sulking. The impact of the extreme situation we witnessed only a short while ago, lightened by its punchline-like ending, is further diminished by the sight of her sitting above him, stroking his head.

The camera tilts to follow her rising in tears. Standing by the bed, Janine's shadow towers over Nick, Robert Saad's chiaroscuro lighting sculpting her body and clothes like a votive figure, while the forest-like lampshade hangs over her right shoulder, to the left of frame, like a comic-strip thought bubble. As she cries 'Why won't you let me help you?!', her sense of thwarted effort is is shadowed by a deeper impression of power: lighting, framing and design are extending the significance of the dramaturgy, with implications that the first-time viewer may find difficult to put their finger on. For the time being, this feeling can be rationalised in terms of the exposition of the scene – she's a threat to Nick's new identity, which he doesn't want her to find out about any more than he wanted her to phone him at work. It's also consistent with the masochistic quality we've noticed in Janine's suffering – a quality which was consciously crafted by Petrie, who famously asked Cronenberg to slap her before every take in which she was to cry.[20] The masochist is always in control, after all, and her emotional energy is greater than her husband's. In retrospect, however, her appearance in this scene will seem as much the beginning of something greater as the parasite activity her arrival interrupted. When Nick uncovers his stomach again after Janine leaves, he watches it begin to pulsate without reacting.

FOOTNOTES

15. Georges Bataille (trans. Mary Dalwood), *Erotism: Death and Sensuality* (San Francisco: City Lights Books, 1986), p. 48.
16. Paul M. Sammon, 'David Cronenberg: Canada's One-Man Horror Industry Shakes Off the Stigma of Being a 'Schlock' Director', *Cinefantastique* Vol. 10 No. 4, Spring 1981, p. 24.
17. Lynn Lowry, interviewed in *Parasite Memories: The Making of 'Shivers'* (Calum Waddell, 2014), Shivers, Arrow Video Blu-Ray release, 2014.
18. Jean-Luc Godard, in Tom Milne (ed.), *Godard on Godard* (New York: Da Capo Press, 1986), p. 173.
19. Manfried Riepe, *Bildgeschwüre Körper und Fremdkörper im Kino David Cronenbergs Psychoanalytische Filmlektüren nach Freud und Lacan* (Bielefeld: Transcript, 2002), p. 21; my translation.
20. Rodley (ed.), p. 48.

Third Reel

13 – Betts' body language

We return to Betts' flat, encountering her alone for the first time in a handheld shot centred on her bed, taken through the bathroom's open doorway. She enters screen space dramatically from the off-screen space behind the rightward bathroom wall, her shadow crossing the bed, where she sits and begins to drink wine. The music, a melodic synthesizer piece which breaks from the downbeat mood of the selections we've heard so far, is interrupted by a startling atonal squall, and we discover that we're hearing a diegetic radio as a male voice begins reading the seven o'clock news. At the announcement, Betts rises quickly and walks into the bathroom, the camera following her to create an extreme low-angle shot of her standing at the bathroom mirror. The bulletin leads with an account of the events in 1511, clarifying that Annabelle was a '19-year-old woman'. The depth of Betts' isolation from the ecosystem outside her rooms is demonstrated by her complete lack of reaction to the news that a murder-suicide took place in the building where she lives. The scene is bifurcated into sound and image, the discrete realities of its material composition. On the image track, Steele's silent performance is a dense collection of flowing body language, conveying a pleasure in movement for its own sake. Betts pours the wine by setting the glass down on the floor between her feet, her legs extended in an A-frame; she jumps up to enter the bathroom, tosses her hair, and makes dynamic use of the dressing gown's sleeves. When she begins to fill the bath, non-diegetic music starts drowning out the next story – a real one, concerning a steelworkers strike – before the water does. As she begins to remove the dressing gown, a last cut takes us back to the bath being filled, as the music rises ominously; with this apparent non-sequitur, the scene ends on its most unnerving disjunction.

In the following scene, Cronenberg again uses image and sound as discrete channels to extend narrative space and alter the significance of the visual information with the context provided by the aural. This time, however, the elements are hinged together in the diegesis by St. Luc's presence, pulled in opposing directions by what each channel is telling him. This is the longest and most structurally complex scene in the film, the turning point of both its narrative and its expositional structure, and it bears examining at length.

The low angle on Betts is followed by an eye-level shot of Forsythe, looking through the folders she's gathered. The room, cropped by the door and apparently small, can permit only one figure to occupy a Hawksian middle-distance shot of professional action, and St. Luc, entering from behind the camera, must take up a position in relation to Forsythe's centrality. In this scene, a shift occurs in our sense of their relationship. Handing him the research he asked for, Forsythe approaches the stereotypical characterisation of the unappreciated secretary pining for her clueless but attractive boss, but the geometry of her relation to his body, Lowry's performance, and our memory of Forsythe's surprising openness to Brad's earlier advances in this clinic, all combine to displace this cliché. She stands over him, maintaining her graphic clarity, while he, hemmed-in and hunched over by the door, is graphically amorphous and reactive. Framed differently, his body language might convey the confidence he seemed to possess when interviewing Janine earlier, but as it is, Forsythe dominates their interpersonal space, leaning in as St. Luc withdraws. Her anger as he answers the phone, and the confident, expectant tone of her approach, were taken by some reviewers to indicate that she's already in a relationship with St. Luc, an implication present at no other point in the film, which is countered by what follows. In a reversal of the expected workplace dynamic of male harasser and female harassed, Forsythe is claiming the privileges of a relationship that St. Luc isn't yet aware of being in. Before we discover what it is, we sense that a kind of life has been happening from which St. Luc is excluded, and thus Cronenberg precedes the revelation of the parasite's nature with the first implication that perhaps whatever 'it' is that's causing these behaviours is simply Eros itself.

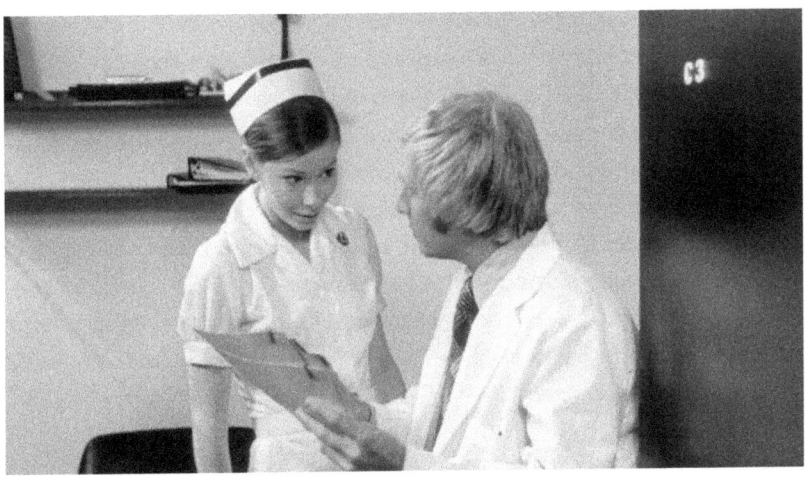

14 – Graphic clarity, reactive posture

As St. Luc answers Linsky's phone call, Forsythe cedes control of the soundtrack. Unseen by St. Luc, she responds with a mime-like facial expression, somewhere between a markedly delayed slow-motion sign of interrupted speech and a fake yawn, consisting only of a wide opening of the mouth, neither believably fatigued nor pointedly sarcastic. At the mid-point of this expression, Lowry makes her face an open-mouthed mask, no longer impatient, but neutrally open, a stylised depiction of hunger as vacancy. In addition to its self-evident vaginal and vampiric resonances, this expression anticipates later narrative and graphic developments in its double allusion to water. Recalling the sculpted animal faces of ornamental fountains' spouts, her mouth looks as likely to pour out something as it is to be filled, although at this point we've yet to learn that the parasite is transmitted by kissing. In Freudian terms, this allusion makes Forsythe's mouth not only vaginal, but also phallic, long before the narrative presents it as a vector of penetration. Secondly, in its resemblance to a fish breathing, it suggests water as immersion, a uterine image in Freud, and foreshadows the site of St. Luc's successful initiation into the community of the infected at the dramatic climax of the film. Via the Freudian correspondences of water to sex and birth, Lowry introduces the nature of the threat in the last possible moment before Linsky's exposition-heavy speech, which will act as a glossing voice-over to Forsythe's subsequent actions, begins.

Forsythe walks out of frame as St. Luc had entered it. St. Luc looks out into offscreen space. The next shot is a medium close-up of Forsythe as she unpins her hat. As in the second part of St. Luc's first meeting with Linsky, Cronenberg has changed the shape of the room by cutting to a previously unseen part of it, in this case shifting the blocking into a new axis which will be maintained throughout the rest of the scene. The composition gives Forsythe plenty of head room, and the lines of her arms are graphically unimpeded by the right angle of the closet behind her. We are on her eye-level, which makes this a mismatch with St. Luc's seated level eyeline. If Forsythe looked up now, she'd be looking over his head and returning the camera's gaze. Although this is a reverse shot, the image track of the narration isn't quite giving us St. Luc's perspective; like Forsythe, it has disengaged from their shared interpersonal space to reach him, and us, in a different register.

As she turns to put her hat away, not looking up at St. Luc, Cronenberg cuts back to him, framed in a tighter close-up. Already, his grip on the phone is looser, and his expression has become less concentrated. From our perspective, Forsythe turning to the wardrobe has rationalised the eyeline mismatch, re-situating his gaze on her body. As we return to see Forsythe turn and reach to unpin her hair in the same framing as her previous shot, Linsky isn't yet coming to the point. Suddenly, we're yanked away by a cut to a close-up of Linsky in his own office, huddled over his desk. High-angle lighting emphasises Joe Silver's cragginess, while the fish tank cuts through his share of the frame, cutting Linsky's body just as St. Luc's office door confines his, both of their postures contrasting with Forsythe's freedom of movement. Linsky's position is given a cruder comic significance on the soundtrack by his declaration that 'Hobbes was shafting us all!' Linsky's movement of Hobbes' papers at the right of the frame and on the soundtrack is answered in the next shot, as St. Luc ruffles the foil in a cigarette packet. His posture is straighter, but his eyes are downcast, avoiding Forsythe. Nonetheless, his vague reply suggests that he's still preoccupied. In the same framing as before, Linsky reveals Hobbes' secret philosophy; Silver's resonant voice and emphatic delivery of 'Man is an *animal* who thinks *too much*' suggest another newsflash. Forsythe has been displaced from the image track, but on the soundtrack, Linsky's lessening of emphasis when not quoting Hobbes' words allows them to resonate as statements, seeming to support her now-unseen efforts.

At the word 'instincts', Cronenberg cuts back to St. Luc, who has returned his gaze to Forsythe's implied position, and now holds a lit cigarette in his free hand, pointed in the same direction. As Linsky says 'too much brain and not enough guts' on the soundtrack, St. Luc nods softly. The combination of classic phallic symbol and comically silent response to a speaker who can only hear him indicate that Forsythe is winning the struggle. At last we return to her. The camera has withdrawn to medium-shot distance in order to frame her action, giving her a larger share of the room's space. Her hair, now loose, conceals her face, channelling our attention towards her hand, which is moving down her stomach (or 'guts'), unbuttoning her uniform and revealing glimpses of her body. As her hand reaches her groin and leaves the bottom of the frame, she returns St. Luc's gaze. For an instant, eroticism transcends its narrative context and dominates the scene – and then Linsky says 'parasite'.

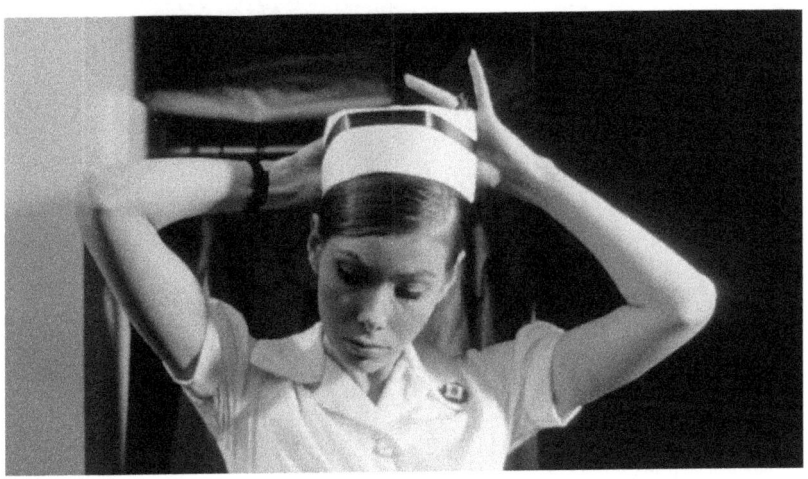

15 – Forsythe unpins

16 – The voice of contested authority

17 – Eroticism transcends narrative

The lexical shift from the figurative to the scientific snags our attention. Cronenberg's cut back to Linsky is immediately followed by his hesitation in reading from Hobbes' notes; his 'uh, here, uh' before resuming teases and exacerbates our frustration as voyeurs more than it does our desire to know what he's about to say. Linsky's use of the

18 – Resisting to focus

19 – Confrontation

word 'aphrodisiac' appears to have an immediate effect; St. Luc frowns as Linsky's voice, following close behind the direct challenge of Forsythe's look, makes sex its own explicit subject. To focus, St. Luc must resist; he's no longer pointing his cigarette in the same direction as his gaze, but smoking it, its role as a Freudian symbol of potency coloured by the introduction of its no less established significance as a repertory shorthand for anxiety. In the shadows cast by his frown, St. Luc's gaze is maintained.

After Linsky is heard saying 'venereal disease', we return to Forsythe. She shifts from her left foot to confront St. Luc more directly with her body, standing parallel to his gaze as she pulls her uniform off, its fabric entering the soundtrack. Parting her lips with an unheard sigh to create a traditional signal of sexual welcome, Lowry briefly softens Forsythe's challenging look with a hint of amusement as Linsky says '… hopefully turn the world into one beautiful, mindless orgy'. As she pulls the uniform from her right arm with a flourish, she lifts and tilts her head, emphasising the height of her standing position relative to St. Luc's perched one. No longer smoking, St. Luc has averted his eyes to concentrate on Linsky's words, but now, not quite believing them, seeks to distance himself from their picture of the situation. His uncommitted half-laugh for Linsky ('sounds a little crazy to me') accompanies the smile he breaks into as he returns his gaze towards Forsythe, seeking to re-establish their shared space. We return to Linsky, who seems to share St. Luc's scepticism, his 'Yeah' given a resigned tone by Silver. Then, with the abruptness of a page turning, Linsky takes control of the scene with a passage of overt expository density. With his announcement that 'the important thing to you, Rog, is this', he seems to acknowledge St. Luc's – and our – divided attention.

His rhetorical question 'You know Annabelle?', with its implication that St. Luc could have forgotten her, returns us to the misogyny of Linsky's earlier dismissive references to her. The male speaker, having displaced the woman's gaze from the image track, underlines the gendered nature of their struggle. Linsky continues: 'Well, he was using her as a guineapig.' On the soundtrack, we hear St. Luc ask 'Guineapig?', his voice enfeebled by the phone receiver effect at the same moment that he's drawn into a passive relationship to Linsky's exposition. But Linsky's reply indicates that his own sense of authority becomes uncertain as he approaches the aspect of the case that most disturbs him. 'Right, now he implanted her with the parasite, and once it took over, well, apparently she, she went berserk.' His stutter over 'she' reveals the extent to which he shares Hobbes' fear of unleashed female sexual agency.

Whether Annabelle consented to her use as guineapig is a question Linsky never addresses, despite her visits to the office he shared with Hobbes. Dealing with her uncontrollable response, and the details of his friend's culpability, Linsky grows ever more uncertain, repeating phrases ('I guess Hobbes wasn't ready for that, so, I guess he just had to kill her'); false-starting ('Well, the p- the point was that – well, he wasn't trying to burn *her*'); finally losing command of his vocabulary ('He was trying to burn… the things, all of them'). St. Luc has fallen into the role of a feed during this shot. We return to find him in a tighter close-up, supporting the resumption of narrative momentum. The sexual meaning of the phrase 'make it', evoked by his reply 'Yeah, well he didn't make it', alludes to the underlying fear in terms of sexual failure. Linsky's turn to act as feed is given dialogue cutting, as the music resumes. Cigarette smoke issuing from St. Luc's mouth as he speaks gives his words graphic weight, yoking the phallic symbol to his authority on the soundtrack. St. Luc softens the blow of the appalling information he has to impart with a provisional recognition both of Hobbes' authority and of Linsky's account, coupled with a stock phrase of slut-shaming: 'Maybe Hobbes didn't know it, but uh, Annabelle Brown was a pretty popular girl around Starliner Towers.' This line, which reminds us of the connection between Annabelle and Brad, and between Brad and Forsythe, seems to confirm our half-suspicion that Forsythe's behaviour on the image track was being associated with the infectious aphrodisiac mentioned on the audio track. When we saw her, Annabelle didn't look any more like the infected residents we've seen so far than Forsythe does. As he says 'I got…', Cronenberg cuts to a slightly high-angle shot of Forsythe's legs as she removes her stockings, implying that St. Luc has dropped his eyes from her gaze, his authority and the threat introduced both permitting and requiring a retreat from scoptophilia to objectification. We hear his voice on the soundtrack switch to a medical lexis, bypassing the origin and nature of the 'growths', asserting control, disclaiming responsibility and censoring the situation from Forsythe's awareness: 'Three men here, maybe four, hosting large, free-moving, apparently pathogenic, ah, abdominal growths that nobody I've tried can identify.' The assertion of control comes with a change of location – 'here' is the building, not the room he and Forsythe currently occupy.

As he speaks, the hissing sound Forsythe's stockings make as she removes them, shriller than her uniform and prominent in the mix, counters his lexical withdrawal with a reach into the soundtrack. Stretching onto tiptoes before beginning to remove her second stocking, she gives this sonic penetration a graphic, vertical echo. The extension of her right leg briefly crosses beyond the bottom of the frame, emphasising its constriction, but also indicating her power to challenge even his averted gaze; his 'ah' occurs as she moves it to the furthest point in its journey. The emergence of her legs from clinical white to their natural flesh tone, in concert with the orange-red carpet beneath her feet and the oscillation of the music, stresses the carnality that St. Luc is evading.

The next shot reveals his gaze once again directed towards with Forsythe, as Linsky summons him back to his professional 'here' on the soundtrack: 'Hey listen, I'd like to come over and take a look at those guys.' As St. Luc begins to arrange their meeting at the Tudors' apartment, his brief look down is no longer evasive, just a resting of the eyes from a position which has become neutral, his smoking now a punctuation to relaxed, professional speech. At the mention of 'Tudor', the music's tense oscillation is replaced by sustained strings. Linsky's reply again brushes over the theme of vision ('Yeah, look, I'll be right over') as a cut back to Forsythe resumes her previous framing, but her right arm, fully extended as she pulls a shirt on, is stretching up out of the frame which previously accommodated her. As Linsky renews his claim to St. Luc's auditory focus ('Er, listen Rog'), Forsythe gathers the shirt at her chest and pulls it down, covering her body. The dark blue of the shirt and her sudden concealment are two kinds of visual cooling, and the colour's darker shadows make her merge with the black rectangle of the closet's sliding door, accentuating her physical distance from St. Luc. Her gaze is unbroken.

On the soundtrack, Linsky's voice falters. A brief shot of St. Luc shows him with a severe expression. Linsky's mention of 'panic' seems to trigger an incongruous harp glissando on the soundtrack, and a cut back to Forsythe after only two seconds confirms that St. Luc's expression was as much a response as much to her action as to the subject of his conversation with Linsky. The glissando, continued over the cut to end on her image, becomes an appropriate introduction for her amused expression as she pulls her shirt down, straightens up and leaves the frame still holding his gaze. The fluency of Linsky's speech is restored by a cut back to him, but the fresh composition he occupies in the new shot subverts his urgency in a different way. Over a third of the frame is now taken up by the water tank, in which a purple-and-white eel is suddenly present, accompanying and upstaging Linsky's speech with a series of abstract graphic shapes, while Silver's right hand, visible through the tank, participates in superimpositions of human and eel movement. The eel's phallic, sensuous qualities make it a stand-in for the parasite, undercutting Linsky's emphatic attempts to overcome his own anxiety with its demonstration of playful, alien intelligence.

Having learned that men are at risk, Linsky now frames Hobbes' culpability in terms of intention rather than accident: 'The way Hobbes designed those things, they get out of hand pretty fast so you gotta be careful' (in a pleasing synchronicity, the eel appears to curl between his fingers as he says 'they get out of hand'). The possibility of himself becoming a victim is raised in the rhetorical 'you' which covers both St. Luc and himself. The line 'I mean, before you even have a chance to know what's happening to you' expresses the horror of lost control absent from his reference to how Annabelle 'went berserk'. Seeking to diminish and neutralise the threat in his own imagination, he uses colloquial language ('that juice'), choosing expressions with an English ring ('the old blood stream… well, I don't know'), which combined with his evident anxiety create a tone unlike his earlier uninhibited style. His reluctance to refer frankly to sex, at a time when clarity is apparently critical ('anything compulsive, I mean any kind of, you know, bizarre sexual things'), reveals his earlier misogynist flippancy as a kind of repression. We return to St. Luc in the same composition as before, pensive and looking down. As Linsky brightens on the soundtrack ('well… once we can get at them, there are a lot of things we can use'), St. Luc looks up into the axis that Forsythe no longer occupies, appearing to consider the possibility of Forsythe's infection, even as his nervous stabbing of the air with his cigarette suggests his suppressed desire to follow her. We return to Linsky, whose confidence has been superficially buoyed by his shift of attention from the fear of infection to the biology of the parasite itself, nonetheless betrays a dramatically ironic subliminal anxiety about his listener's lack of response ('Maybe we'd start with a kind of a, a basic tropical kit and work up from there, uh?'); now that nothing else is happening to St. Luc, Linsky's words imply the recognition that something else might be. Without waiting for a reply, Linsky ends the scene with his injunction to 'get at them. And fast.'

During this scene, we've been offered a non-narrative visual pleasure only to hear it get swallowed by the narrative. Yet, like the parasite converting its hosts, Forsythe's image has changed the machine that ingested it. By coupling visual pleasure to aural infodump, Cronenberg not only smooths our experience of a passage of pure exposition, but also qualifies our enjoyment in a way that produces a comic shudder. Is the suddenness of

Forsythe's display a sign of her infection? Is our delight in its blatancy a sign of ours? Scott Wilson's baffling claims that 'the sequence is utterly devoid of any kind of eroticism',[21] and that 'neither of the diegetic gazes (St. Luc's or Forsythe's) carry any hint of arousal and so neither can ours', quite apart from their inattentiveness to Cronenberg's sounds and images, also indicate a faulty grasp of the poetics of exploitation cinema. If we consider this scene tin he context of exploitation film spectatorship, it's clear that the main reason Forsythe's strip makes no material difference to St. Luc's behaviour is that St. Luc is not the primary audience: we are. It requires no response from the watching doctor, nor any plausible behavioural rationale; our presumed desire to see her do it is enough. After all, no female nudity has appeared for twenty-nine minutes, and Lowry is attractive. Watching Forsythe watching St. Luc watch her, we're happy for the narrative to be de-prioritised at the very point that it begins to gain urgency, and this is how its ostensible values begin to be subverted. Because the fight against the parasites gives St. Luc an alibi for not responding to Forsythe's advances, our own voyeurism predisposes us to take the parasites' side. An indication of Forsythe's triumph, and that of the parasites, is the tendency of critics and analysts discussing this scene to refer to her as St. Luc's 'girlfriend', despite the film's obscurity over this point.[22] (Most obviously, St. Luc doesn't know her first name.)

Cronenberg has stated that St. Luc's lack of response to Forsythe's advances was intended to indicate an indifference to sexuality: 'There's a repressed sexual something going on. He's a saint, don't forget. He doesn't really get close to her, to kiss her, until the disease has introduced itself.'[23] The performance of Paul Hampton introduces noise into this signal; St. Luc seems too at ease with himself to be credible as sexually repressed. When Forsythe kisses him, he doesn't reciprocate, but neither does he seem uncomfortable. His preoccupied affect is often very funny, but it's a character detail on a leading man; the preoccupation and the asexuality aren't credibly integrated components of a coherent personality, as they'll be in Jeff Goldblum's performance as Seth Brundle in Cronenberg's later film, *The Fly* (1986). Like Lowry, Hampton is American, which complicates things further. If Cronenberg had cast a French Canadian actor, St. Luc's name, and the film's setting in Montreal, could have permitted our reading him as a Catholic refraining from pre-marital intercourse. As Cronenberg's words indicate, the choice of name is itself a Catholic reference, St. Luke being the patron saint of doctors, surgeons, artists, students and butchers – a Cronenbergian bundling.

The association of a desiring female subject with fear raises the question of whether we're watching a misogynist film. To mistake the comic ripple of fear created by the juxtaposition of Forsythe's strip and Linsky's revelations for an expression of simple misogyny would be to miss the pleasure in Cronenberg's unease. If women frighten him on some level, then it's a fear he enjoys and uses; he writes and stages scenes which allow them to be as magnetic and as powerful as possible, and these images are as available for women's use as they are for anyone else's. Cronenberg's account of how, during filming, Barbara Steele pushed him against a wall and lifted him off the ground is evidently told with a certain amount of recalled excitement.[24] Our answer to the question of whether this kinky, complex fear should be classified as a cerebral form of misogyny depends on how far we are willing to go along with Angela Carter's assertion that men's eroticised awe of women is merely an awe of their own erections.[25] Many sado-masochists and Goddess-worshippers would dispute this reading.

The dialogue between Linsky and St. Luc in this scene was the only explanation we'll ever hear of what's going on at Starliner Tower. From here onwards, our protagonists' struggle to escape carries us from one appalling image or encounter to another: when it becomes most linear and concentrated, *Shivers* is closest to being non-narrative in its appeal.

Earlier, we saw the epigraph '"Sex is the invention of a clever venereal disease." – Emil Hobbes', taped to the fridge behind Linsky, reminding us of the first quotation we saw, William Blake's 'The road of excess leads to the palace of wisdom'. Now we learn its diegetic significance. Hobbes' secret project is an irrational, romantic intrusion into science, and our memory of Blake's words accompanied the account we heard from Linsky. Despite Herbert Marcuse's analysis of 'repressive desublimation'[26] in his 1964 work *One-Dimensional Man*, the process by which the radical potential of liberated sexuality was recuperated into capitalism by the advertising industry, the undertheorised equation of sexual revolution with political revolution had become entrenched in New Left thinking. The most popularly influential psychoanalyst was the paranoid schizophrenic pseudoscientist Wilhelm Reich, while the most popularly influential psychiatrist was R. D. Laing, who held that paranoid schizophrenia didn't exist – a lucky break for Reichians. Their work was taken to provide scientific justification for the culture's general, unexamined conviction that the notion that anyone's desires could cause harm should be dismissed as the voice of an inner capitalist-patriarchical censor. (That Reich, dead since 1957, had been a Republican-voting anti-communist in life was no obstacle to this posthumous deployment.) The attempt to reconcile utopian libertarianism and utopian Marxism had resulted in an unacknowledged relapse of vulgar Rousseauvianism, of which the most conspicuous example was the regime of Pol Pot, who took power in Cambodia a few months before Shivers was released in Canada. The suppression of desire was a capitalist evil; liberate desire and society's cure would begin.

Until that liberation could be achieved, rationality itself would be in question. Laing, Reich and their fellow secular gurus of the period were surely an influence on Cronenberg's institutional mad scientists, whose personality cults and institutional support systems shield their abuses from exposure, and whose author knows that secular gurus are, as a profession, finally no more secular than Stalinists. If, putting aside Cronenberg's own Canadian liberalism, we decide to consciously misread *Shivers* as a left political statement, we discover a warning against the dangers of seeking an ideologically incoherent 'passion' for social ends while leaving false consciousness untouched – a warning perfectly compatible with that of Marcuse eleven years earlier. We could even consider this a timely intervention for the mid-point of the chrysalis decade in which former hippies evolved into proto-yuppies. The cognitive dissonance between libertarianism and Marxism ended with the victory of libertarian capitalism in the elections of Thatcher and Reagan, whose common ideology dispensed with the aspiration to social cohesion that had characterised social conservatisms of the past – a change which felt revolutionary to its adherents.

Returning to the worldview I've characterised as 'Canadian liberalism', let's consider the political circumstances of Cronenberg's own formation. When *Shivers* was released, Canada's Liberal Party had been in power for all but six years of his life, and this dominance was typical of its history: the subsequent twelve-year period in opposition between 2003 and 2015 was the longest it had spent out of power since 1896. The coherence of Canada as a nation, composed as it is of four distinct territories, depends upon a degree of mutual tolerance. Quebec's situation is well-known, and Newfoundland had been a separate dominion until 1949. Notions of stability associated with reactionary positions in homogeneous cultures must be read more sympathetically when they appear as the aspiration of a fragmented society. Canada is the arbitrary result of imperialism, only recently required to imagine a coherent sense of itself; this has made its film culture even more prey than Britain's has been to the nonsense of 'national cinema' – a concept which, entailing as it does the distortion and suppression of cultural plurality and individual vision, has only ever served the interests of Hollywood. Cronenberg's own arbitrarily essential Canadianness points up the arbitrariness of coming from anywhere else; Cronenberg is Canadian because it was important for him not to let being Canadian limit him, and leaving Canada would imply the recognition that it had been a limit. By never becoming American, he has remained to some extent a citizen of the world, inhabiting both American and European contexts; staying in the provinces has preserved him from provincialism.

The most significant negative evaluations of the film remain those offered by Robert Fulford and Robin Wood. Fulford was a fixture of the Canadian cultural scene, while Wood, British when he first wrote about Shivers, had become Canadian by the last time he wrote about it.

Writing as 'Marshall Delaney' for the middlebrow *Saturday Night*,[27] Fulford adhered to the values of film society-based, small-canon liberal humanist film criticism, for which low-budget realism was virtue, low-budget fantasy was vice, and a commercial film was always an example of something, never an object in itself. The threat of Hollywood kept these biases current for longer in Canada than in America or Europe, and not only among those who couldn't be expected to know better; as late as the 1980s, John Grierson's strictures were being deferred to in Cinema Canada, the trade magazine of the English-Canadian film industry. *Shivers*, which Fulford reviewed under its original title *The Parasite Murders*, represented to him both an un-Canadian aberration and a misuse of public funds. It also afforded him with an opportunity to hit back against the influence of auteurism on the evaluation of popular cinema as art: '... a school of filmmaking and film connoisseurship that focuses its attention on a chic version of junk filmmaking.'

Fulford makes traditional sheep-and-goats divisions. Among the sheep, 'avant-garde filmmakers' and 'a few artists – people like Peter Pearson, Don Shebib, Allan King – who wanted to speak seriously to audiences of some size'; among the goats, 'filmmakers of little talent and inspiration seeking to pander to mass audiences on the lowest terms'. For a filmmaker of great talent and inspiration to speak seriously to a mass audience was, for a critic with this outlook, categorically impossible. Fulford had praised Cronenberg for *Stereo*; now, in a passage of bitter armchair psychology, he suggested he had 'become a commercial movie-maker with very little talent'. In moving, as I've put it, from the cathedral of experimental film to the garage of exploitation movies, Cronenberg had defected from one camp to the other.

Fulford's article was of use in the promotion of Shivers; tellingly, the piece is now only readily available as part of a promotional booklet preserved on Cinepix's website.[28] The director had previewed the film to Fulford personally, apparently expecting him to appreciate it. Had Fulford's piece been merely a virulent pan, it might have worked more straightforwardly for promotional purposes, establishing the kind of viewer Cronenberg's film *wasn't* for. It was Fulford's incorporation of his review within a broader criticism of government policy that his piece threatened the progress of Cronenberg's career, as indeed seems to have been Fulford's intention. Fortunately, the impact of the piece was short-lived, and the funding policy that had made *Shivers* possible was maintained. Within a few years, this would lead to the production boom of the 'tax shelter' era, from which Cronenberg would benefit.

Robin Wood's evaluation of the film was to have a more lasting, international impact. At this point, *Shivers* requires no defence; as Steven Shaviro noted, '[i]t is not Cronenberg, but Wood, who responds to the sexual monstrosity in which the film revels with phobic disgust, and who regards this monstrosity as an objection to the life of the body'.[29]

Nonetheless, the terms of Wood's attacks are worth examining for what they reveal about the film's relation to its cultural context.

Wood's major weaknesses as a critic were his impatience with nuance and his inability to process ambiguity; the inflexible thinking which famously led him to miss the point of *Belle de Jour* (Luis Buñuel 1967) during his bourgeois humanist period wasn't remedied by his later personal and ideological shifts, merely turned upon different objects. Moving from a 'bourgeois humanist' orthodox Leavisite position to a 'Marxist', gay but equally orthodox Leavisite position, he pivoted, and changed his adjectives of approval and disapproval, but never defined his terms any more rigorously, or moved beyond an appeal to the implicit assumptions he expected his readers to share.

Reading the Edinburgh Film Festival report in which Wood first damned *Shivers*,[30] we find Cronenberg in good company, with Straub-Huillet, Michael Snow and Joyce Wieland, among others, receiving contemptuous, occasionally philistine treatment. Much of the piece appears to be a passive-aggressive attack on the selection policy of the Festival's organisers. After faulting most of their choices, Wood concluded the piece by calling *The Enigma of Kasper Hauser* (Werner Herzog, 1975) and *Wrong Move* (Wim Wenders, 1975) two of the 'most impressive achievements of the festival', revealing how bourgeois his standards remained. The sophistication of *Shivers* seems to have taken Wood by surprise; seeing it as an expression of 'extreme sexual disgust', he missed the point of the ending. Wood failed to pick up on the film's shifting attitude to the parasites until the climax of the film; once he noticed it, he thought it was a mistake, wondering 'whether Cronenberg realized that it could be read as a happy ending'.[31] That he thought something so obvious could be unintentional suggests a faulty grasp of the material realities of filmmaking unforgivable in a critic seeking to engage with dialectical materialism.

Wood's discussion of Cronenberg in the introduction to *American Nightmare* (1975) is mercifully brief, two paragraphs en route to a more extensive condemnation of John Carpenter, and is important mainly because the book's publication brought about the extraordinary, and very Canadian, situation of Cronenberg and Wood being brought together for an on-stage discussion. The paragraph on *Shivers* repeats the incomprehension of his 1975 dismissal with rhetorical inflation: 'extreme sexual disgust' is elaborated into 'unmitigated horror'.[32] A satisfyingly assertive phrase, but as we've seen, quite incorrect.[33]

In his last and most sustained consideration of the director's work, 'David Cronenberg: A Dissenting View', written in 1983,[34] Wood, despite having heard and read Cronenberg spell out the meaning of the ending, doubles down on his original claim, insisting that Cronenberg *couldn't* have intended it that way. In view of Wood's commitment to close reading, and the regularity with which he modified or retracted previous conclusions in print throughout his career, his unwillingness to revise his earlier misreading – even at the cost of making himself absurd – is remarkable.

In valuing horror films chiefly for their capacity to express political ideas of which he approved, Wood had effectively reverted to the pre-auteurist model which approved of cinema itself only to the extent that it could act as an effective carrier of improving values to a mass audience; he was closer to Fulford's liberal humanist values than he would have wished to recognise. Wood's weak deflection that Cronenberg's films could only be called superior to those of Tobe Hooper or his other favourites by appeal to 'the long-discredited criterion of the bourgeois "well-made film"',[35] quite apart from its being untrue, fails to conceal the fact that his own preferences were formed in the matrix of bourgeois well-*meaning* film criticism. If the discussion isn't finally about aesthetics, it's about nothing; nobody is going to become more revolutionary because of a few chuckles of classist sarcasm about the nuclear family in *The Texas Chain Saw Massacre* (Tobe Hooper, 1974), and the underlying hope of Wood's Marxist Freudianism – that the right films might persuade people to love the revolution more than their families – reflects a misanthropic naivety gone with the wind. Not only the appeal, but the credibility of this way of thinking is becoming more difficult to reconstruct in our imaginations as time goes on.

Why did Wood spend eight years defending his incomprehension of a film he had misunderstood? The issue, as it had been with *Belle de Jour*, was his need to claim systematicity for a defensive emotional response. Wood's ideas about repression drew heavily from Reich, as the opening section of his introduction to *American Nightmare* makes plain,[36] and we've seen what Cronenberg made of Reich – Hobbes, an advocate of irrational libidinous release who's self-deceiving, disingenuous and mentally ill. Wood never addressed *Shivers*, or any of Cronenberg's work, in terms of an address to specific ideas, but he revealed the underlying intellectual issue in two passing phrases. Firstly, when cataloguing *Shivers*' depictions of sexuality, Wood uses the misjudged euphemism 'age difference'[37] for paedophilia, obviously in defence of the Reichian pseudoscience about 'child sexuality' restated in his introduction. Secondly, in 'A Dissenting View', Wood writes of *Scanners* and *Videodrome* that 'the ambition of the scientist... has far less progressive connotations, so that the "awful warning" the films offer is less unacceptable'.[38] In other words, the heart of Wood's objection to *Shivers* is that he considers Hobbes an insulting depiction of a progressive. This reading is only tenable in the presence of two other conclusions. Firstly, the viewer must interpret Hobbes as a representation of Reich-as-cultural-totem rather than Reich-as-thinker; secondly, the viewer must believe that a project of mass rape is assimilable to a valid revolutionary praxis. If Wood had reached the first conclusion, he never argued for it, and if he had reached the second, then his problem with Shivers was that it wasn't sick *enough*. However he rationalised it, coherent ideology is nowhere in Wood's reactive evaluation.

We return to Betts' bathroom. The action that follows was a long-standing fantasy of Cronenberg's; he had first used it, in a de-eroticised form, in his experimental short *From the Drain* (1967). The image's origin as a dream or fantasy is detectable in the detail that the bath never drains after the parasite's body has crawled clear of the plughole, the breach of physics going unnoticed by the dreaming mind in its fascination with the image.

The strong horizontal line provided by the side of the bath makes the camera's canted angle obvious; this seems too slight to be the expression of a definite aesthetic intention, but whatever the circumstances of its creation, it tips Betts' legs towards the plughole in a graphic anticipation. In close up, she presses the glass against her face and her lips again as we saw her and opens her eyes in an inward, melancholic expression. Combined with her solitude and nudity, the handheld tremor of this first facial close-up merges the vulnerability of character and star. A brief shot establishes the plughole as a location before we return to see the nose of the parasite emerging. The parasite is depicted by the same finger puppet seen coming out of the Tudors' letterbox earlier. This time, the effect is comic. Cronenberg begins a pattern of suspense cutting between Betts and the parasite, using the ripples of the water to create the illusion of movement when we see it mid-journey. Oblivious, Betts' expression suggests sexual reverie. As a rape fantasy, the parasite's attack on Betts incorporates self-debasement, as the fantasist seeking to use it must be willing to enter into the identity of a bodiless penis. If we treat this identification in concrete terms – as Cronenberg's materialist approach seems to demand – it belongs equally to the genre of giantess fantasy. Her hair, flowing gown and dominant personality have already made her a 'phallic woman', in Freudian terms, and the outcome of this attack is a repurposing of the myth of vagina dentata: her vagina receives and retains the phallus.

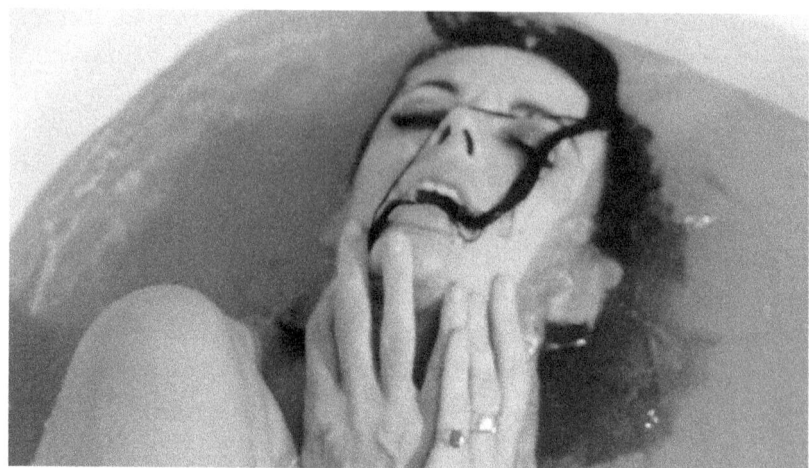

20 – Betts infected

Cut to Forsythe waiting for St. Luc by the clinic door. St. Luc no longer resists nor seems uninterested in her advances, in fact they now seem like a couple, as if something has been consummated or confirmed. He accepts a supper invitation from her, but chooses not to tell her about the parasites. His decision to restrict her knowledge will soon have dire consequences; if we need a sense of vengeance to justify the pleasure we take in his eventual fate, this moment provides it.

Forsythe emerges from an outer door into the lobby, in a shot which demonstrates Cronenberg's architectural eye; using the line of the wall to create a strong diagonal, ending in a glass wall. This shot begins a pattern of shooting the lobby from the opposite side to that seen during the daytime scenes, moving the body of the building from our right to our left. This space, already the aesthetic highlight of the building, looks better with artificial lighting. On the soundtrack, a strong and steady wind forms a bed for Forsythe's loud, echoing footsteps; rather than the stormy nights of classic horror, which it echoes, this wind suggests a bare, cold landscape – the inhospitable nature feared by Northrop Frye's 'garrison mentality'. Like a garrison, the building seems to be coming into its own now that it's under attack, and for the moment, the wind heightens our sense of its isolation. Back at the clinic door, St. Luc is pensive.

In Betts' bath, the dream-like suspension of physics has ended, and the water has drained away. A handheld shot of Steele's feet is accompanied by the sound of her breathing. The erotic intimacy of the breathing is modified by the unglamorous fleshiness of the feet; their unpainted nails, seen in the cold white light of the bathroom, suggest a corpse in a morgue. The redemption of all flesh has begun. A close-up with a narrow band of focus shows the feet landing in the shards of her wine glass and walking out of frame. (The power of this image is only slightly muted by our noticing that the soles of Steele's feet have been painted red prior to her stepping on the glass.)

The director provides a voice-over which the sound mix situates in diegetic space: 'Delivery for 416 from Felipe's restaurant.' As Delivery Boy (Charles Perley), whose voice this is, enters the lobby, his ornate trolley sticks on the threshold. This comic beat invites us to savour the absurd contrast between the gentility of the trolley's presentation and the geometric starkness of the environment. Once again, exile and incongruity are associated with Betts, whose delivery this is. Appearing confined by his uniform, Perley isn't ideal casting for a waiter, but for a man working as a waiter, he's existentially ideal.

We've seen four infected people: Annabelle, Nick, Brad and (from the ankles down) Betts, none of whom behaved in the frenzied way Linsky warned St. Luc and us to expect. Within horror fandom, *Shivers* is often discussed as an honorary zombie film, although instances of the infected behaving like zombies are infrequent. The return of the Laundry Woman now, just over halfway through the film, is *Shivers*' first example of zombie-like behaviour. Her single phrase is discreet and old-fashioned: 'I'm hungry for love!' From this, and from her heavy make-up, we conclude that the parasite impels only the forms of expression comfortable to the infected person, with civilised social responses not abolished, as we might have expected, but used as part of its own expression. Later developments complicate this provisional conclusion. Her attack on the delivery boy is the first assault we see committed by one of the infected, and is played as physical comedy.

Linsky is looking through black-and-white topless photographs of Annabelle as he prepares to take the Hobbes papers to Starliner Tower. He takes a long look at each photograph, even turning one around to enjoy it in landscape orientation. His own shot continues the framing seen at the end of his phone call with St. Luc, making this moment a cynical postscript to that exchange. Five minutes after Forsythe got dressed, his pleasure in looking provides an opportunity for our own. Silver passes a couple of empty Coke cans as he leaves the shot, and Cronenberg lets Silver's journey through off-screen space change the light on them and the fish tank before cutting; thus the element of the composition most determined by pragmatism is redeemed by an expression of pure joy in form.

Forsythe is preparing the meal. She's changed into a black evening dress, which she'll be wearing for most of the rest of the film. Apart from Betts' sewing – and as we've established, Betts is a special case – we haven't seen anyone exercising a skill until now. While the other apartments have surrounded their occupants with a great deal of negative space, the dimensions of Forsythe's kitchen place everything within her arm's reach. As with Betts' apartment, the dense mass of tiny signs comprehended in this space imply a greater individuation of personhood; more is more. Where we might

21 – Forsythe at home

expect to see a clock, Forsythe has hung a happy-looking anthropomorphic cartoon sun, with pink lips, red blushing cheeks and long eyelashes. After so many handheld close-ups, we notice the use of a tripod in the arcing motion of this shot, and appreciate the precise work required of the focus puller. Lowry's performance of Forsythe's contentment may make the line 'It's lovely' seem superfluous, a rare instance of its writer-director erring on the side of the written word, but it conveys the security of her happiness. This is destroyed by the knock on the door. Her defensive stance with the carving fork is a foreshadowing, and also suggests prescience on her part; we remember our uncertainty about how much she already knows. It's also social realism – she's a woman alone in her apartment, and the knock was a 'policeman's knock', male and aggressive.

In a new tripodded shot, Forsythe opens the door to reveal Kresimer Sviben, the bland young man we saw arriving with his pregnant wife at the start of the film. After they served to inject us into the building's bloodstream, we lost sight of them, and his abrupt reappearance alone may make us wonder what's happened to her. Cronenberg's later record of uterine horror, in *Scanners*, *The Fly* and *Dead Ringers* (1988), the last of which he had already begun writing at the time of *Shivers*' shooting, suggests that squeamishness is unlikely to have been a factor, yet as we'll soon see, this unrepresentability of the infected mother relates to a pattern of circumspection.

Sviben seems disturbed, holding on to the entrance of the apartment across the corridor. Immediately, we realise he has not come seeking help. The camera tracks backwards and pans, emphasising the spatial continuity of the public corridor and the private space, as Sviben forces his way into Forsythe's apartment and begins trying to rape her. A cut to a low-level shot begins a quick-cut struggle.

During the next twenty-five minutes, we'll see six depictions of rape or attempted rape; this is the first, and a second attack on Forsythe will be the last. These differ from the Laundry Woman's attack in their serious tone and relative naturalism: the attackers are men, the victims are women. None of these acts of violence are eroticised, and mainstream films like *Straw Dogs* (Sam Peckinpah, 1971) and *High Plains Drifter* (Clint Eastwood, 1973) had gone further in both detail and prurience. Rape, associated in those films, as in many others, with 'untameable' male individuality, signifies in *Shivers* a dissolving of individuation which makes volition irrelevant. Although the film's action implies that most such attacks result in infection, Cronenberg cuts away from the only two that 'succeed' in transmitting the parasite. Some commentators have taken the second attack on Forsythe as the point at which she becomes infected, but this is by no means clear; the timeline of her infection remains ambiguous.

During Sviben's attack, Cronenberg's direction of Lowry's post-syncing introduces a note of unreality, as her voice punctuates the struggle with reserved 'ooh's and 'um's; rather than leavening the grimness of what we see on the image track, this creates an impression of directorial detachment which makes the scene more difficult to watch. What's happening here? Almost as soon as we've learned what the infection is, we're shown that the infected don't behave consistently. Sviben has no zombie-phrase or scarring, he appears to be simply a disturbed rapist. The sequence of quick cuts ends with Forsythe stabbing Sviben in the shoulder with the carving fork and running out of the apartment.

Linsky is leaving for Starliner Tower. This is the film's only exterior shot of a building other than Tourelle-Sur-Rive. What we can make out of it is dark, ornate stone, a strong contrast to Linsky's destination.[39] We see Linsky wave to someone at a distance to his right, a bit of business which suggests the presence of the collegiate community the film has no time or money to depict, as well as balancing the sleaziness we saw in his previous scene with a reminder of his warm personal manner. His size in the frame, and the chilly atmosphere created by the greenish glass of the door and the dark stone of the building, make him appear vulnerable. Heightening this impression is his long white car, the brightest point in the darkness of a courtyard of which we see little but the surrounding windows.

In a new composition of the internal door we saw before, St. Luc is leaving the clinic. After the shadows of the previous two shots, the bright light in this space, showing up the irregularities in the surface of the glossy black door, is glaring. Forsythe rushes in and throws her arms around him; seeing her emotional state as she recounts the incident we've just seen, he maintains the embrace, comforting her. The parasite has brought them together. Our sense of the threat is escalated by our recognition that neither staying at the clinic nor following St. Luc seems a safer course of action.

We return to Forsythe's apartment before St. Luc arrives, and with no human figures in the frame, we're given space and time to notice the most '70s kitsch' interior decoration we've seen, with a zebra-print breakfast bar to match the covering we see on the television at the frame's left edge, and the leather chair into which Forsythe fell. These choices have diegetic significance as further examples of Forsythe's taste. Where the furnishings in Annabelle and the Tudors' apartments indicated a desire to import 'primitive' aesthetics into an antiseptic environment, Forsythe's choices bring signifiers of vitality and nature directly into the home. The boldness with which kitsch aesthetics claim the emotional associations of their allusions is what makes them socially embarrassing. Forsythe's bold embrace of vulgarity, and the specific allusions her choices make, provide us with further indications of her unnoticed strength. Considered in this light, the feminine features of the anthropomorphic sun on her kitchen wall, half-visible in this shot, take on a deeper significance. This second, more explicit solar figure counters the earlier association of Sol with the aggressive hubris of Hobbes. Solar deities have generally been male; this feminine Sol, in its association with Forsythe, foreshadows the deeper revolution which lies ahead.

22 – *Fragments of a parasite*

Sviben has contaminated the room: along with scattered underwear on the floor (suggesting paraphilia), we see blood and what appear to be fragments of parasite. A tap running in the bathroom off-screen reminds us of the most recent parasite attack, turning our minds back to the source of the threat after the more realistic assault we've just witnessed. The bathroom's open doorway creates mild unease, until St. Luc turns the tap off without encountering either Sviben or another plumbing-borne parasite. A brief close-up of the bloody carving fork on the floor sets up the next shock.

Cronenberg cuts from a tripodded low-angle close shot of St. Luc's hands putting the samples into a test tube to a shaky handheld close-up of him looking down. The camera angle and the texture of the movement, seen so soon after the shot of the bloody fork, give us the impression he's being watched, which indeed turns out to be the case. Having essayed the post-*Psycho* build-up and release earlier, Cronenberg tries his hand at the false-alarm jump scare with the sudden crash of a pan falling onto the floor. Apologetic, Forsythe seems suddenly recovered, and her unexpected cheerfulness qualifies our relief. We've already felt uncertain about her connection to the infected; *was* this a false alarm, after all? The happy sun is over her shoulder. St. Luc smiles in the same handheld set-up as before, detaching the camera's point-of-view from its passing identification with that of Forsythe.

The Guilbaults are the next residents to encounter a parasite. This one is black and wet, resembling both a glutted leech and a bloody stool; with comic meanness, Cronenberg has taken us from an aural reminder of food to a visual reminder of faeces. As it crawls up the leg of Mrs. Guilbault's walker, the parasite's wet, shiny blackness is echoed by her patent leather shoes and contrasted by the metal's brightness, evoking surgery's thrilling contrast of hygienic medical steel and hot viscera. The parasite travels faster when off-screen – there's a strong mismatch between the direction of Mrs. Guilbault's gaze when she first sees it and its proximity to her when it begins attacking a moment later. Suddenly, it's on the walker; when we cut back to her almost immediately, she's now looking straight down at it. Its impossible speed between shots, and her inexplicable stasis, suggest the action of a nightmare. A sense of visceral 'presence' is restored by the squelching thuds we hear on the soundtrack as Mr. Guilbault attacks the parasite with the rubber end of the walker.

Janine is reading her magazine and smoking. A vase of flowers draws our attention to the unused dinner table which, like the bedroom lampshade earlier, is positioned like a thought bubble behind her. We are reminded of the date she isn't keeping with Betts, and notice that Janine has changed her clothes, now wearing a floral-patterned skirt. Within a few seconds, Petrie and Cronenberg create a poignant image of disappointment. That this naturalistic, minor-key emotion reaches us so sharply, despite the spectacular horrors either side of it, may serve as a rebuttal to the frequent misreading of Cronenberg as a 'cold' director. Janine turns on the television; this doesn't disrupt the lighting, but fills the soundtrack with a romantic exchange in French-accented English. We hear the dialogue continue faintly over the next shot.

Nick convulses in bed as the parasites in his stomach move, the sudden loudness of his post-synchronised gasp giving us a start. (The staging of this effects shot was reportedly influenced by Joe Blasco's desire to prove to his colleagues that he hadn't used a false stomach to execute the stomach 'lumps'.) Janine, restless, turns the television back off after a brief attempt to watch it and read her magazine at the same time. In view of Janine's frustration and her husband's earlier unpleasantness, there's an unexpected satisfaction for the viewer in the cruel elegance with which the director has contrived to have Nick's cry remain unheard.

As the film's opening theme begins playing again, Forsythe and St. Luc walk down a semi-darkened hallway towards us, talking about reporting the attack to the doorman. For this exchange, Lowry and Hampton use a line delivery that sounds more improvised than we've heard from them so far, Hampton breaking one line with what sounds like real hesitancy. On the soundtrack, we hear them approaching the microphone from the edge of its range as they approach the camera, the direct recording adding a breath of documentary materiality to the escalating fantasy of the diegesis. Cronenberg repeats his trick of cutting from depth staging to flat surfaces, filling most of the screen's expanse with the black rectangle of an elevator door.

Seen in profile while they wait for the elevator, there's a comic contrast between Forsythe's depressed, tired energy and St. Luc's attempt at a comforting smile. Despite possessing the fuller knowledge of what's happening at Starliner Tower, St. Luc seems confident that the situation can be kept under control; if he's made the connection between this attack and the behaviour Linsky warned him to look out for, he hasn't mentioned it to Forsythe. At this point, we recall how wrong he was about Nick during Janine's appointment. Evidence of the wider danger arrives when the elevator door opens to reveal the Guilbaults.

23 – *The Guilbaults*

While Mr. Guilbault tells St. Luc the story, Cronenberg cuts in for an appreciative close-up of Mrs. Guilbault's burn, surrounded by the texture of her skin, which St. Luc shifts and ripples as her examines her. Hampton's hands are in softer focus than Posnanska's arm and its burn make-up, and exploitation film spectatorship comes in again here. This scene provides us with three important pieces of information, one graphic and two expositional. Because we're as interested in spectacle as we are in narrative, we're given a beat to enjoy the graphic information before a cut back to the previous shot underlines Mr. Guilbault's answer that he put the parasite 'In the chute, in the garbage.' The film's way of looking at bodies, and thus our way of seeing them, seems once again to be being inflected by the carnal vision of the parasite.

As St. Luc asks Mr. Guilbault for their apartment number, the soundtrack continues over an exterior leftward pan, at a high elevation. The shot takes in the city lights across the river and the lighted windows of the building, through some of which Tourelle-Sur-Rive's real residents can be glimpsed. This is a beautiful interlude of light, colour and movement, a non-narrative pleasure, although the oscillating music cue we heard earlier is laid over it to create tension. Here we have our first indication of the director's visionary transformation of the location: we see nothing frightening, and nothing staged or acted, but we accept that this juxtaposition of music and image represents the transmission of the parasites throughout the building. We cut back to the same shot at the elevator for the second and last important piece of exposition: St. Luc wants Forsythe to wait with the Guilbaults. As St. Luc runs down the corridor we saw before, the sound of the elevator door closing on the soundtrack underlines the diegetic continuity of the two spaces.

FOOTNOTES

21. Scott Wilson, *The Politics of Insects* (New York: Continuum, 2011), p. 43.
22. See for example Richard Combs' review in *Monthly Film Bulletin*, March 1976, p. 62, in which he refers to her as St. Luc's 'nurse/girlfriend', and William Beard's comment '...despite her apparent status St. Luc's "girlfriend"...' (Beard, p. 42).
23. William Beard, Piers Handling, 'The Interview', in Piers Handling (ed.), *The Shape of Rage: The Films of David Cronenberg* (Toronto: The Academy of Canadian Cinema, 1983), p. 178.
24. Rodley (ed.), p. 50.
25. Angela Carter, *The Sadeian Woman: An Exercise in Cultural History* (London: Virago Press, 1979), p. 7.
26. Herbert Marcuse, *One-Dimensional Man: Studies in the Ideology of Advanced Industrial Society* (London: Routledge, 2002), p. 76.
27. The source of all that Fulford quotes that follow is Marshall Delaney [Robert Fulford], 'You Should Know How Bad This Film Is. After All, You Paid For It.', in *Saturday Night* (September 1975), pp. 83-85.
28. *Is There A Place for Horror Films In Canada's Film Industry?*, apparently compiled by the General Sales Manager of Cinépix, the wonderfully-named Orval Fruitman, can be accessed at http://www.cinepix.ca/downloads/12/Shivers - Article - Cinepix responds to critics - Reaction Piece.pdf.
29. Steven Shaviro, 'Bodies of Fear: The Films of David Cronenberg', in Brian Massumi, (ed.), *The Politics of Everyday Fear* (Minneapolis: University of Minnesota Press, 1993), p. 118.
30. Robin Wood, 'New Cinema at Edinburgh', *Film Comment*, November/December 1975, pp. 25-29.
31. Ibid., p. 26.
32. Robin Wood, 'An Introduction to the American Horror Film', in Andrew Britton et al, *American Nightmare: Essays on the Horror Film* (Toronto: Festival of Festivals, 1979), p. 24.
33. For a detailed examination of the distortions created by placing Cronenberg in the context of 'the American nightmare', see Gaile McGregor's essay 'Grounding the Countertext: David Cronenberg and the Ethnospecificity of Horror', in *Revue Canadienne d'Études*

cinématographiques / Canadian Journal of Film Studies Vol. 2, No. 1 (Spring/printemps 1992), pp. 43-62.

34. Handling (ed.), p. 115-36.
35. Ibid., p. 118.
36. Wood in Britton, pp. 7-9.
37. Ibid., p. 24.
38. Wood in Handling ed., p. 129.
39. The role of this unnamed teaching hospital appears to have been played by a building at the Royal Victoria Hospital of Montreal, whose Department of Immunology and Microbiology is thanked in the film's credits.

Fourth Reel

Having followed St. Luc's run into distant screen space, our eyes are hit by Joe Silver's bright, slightly-out-of-focus jaw as Linsky eats *en route*, reminding us of his first scene with a guerilla roughness that recalls our mixed feelings about him. A brief shot of his long white car driving down a road in Montreal gives us a breath of city air.

An insert shot of an elevator's floor indicator lights suggests that Forsythe and the Guilbaults are about to be waylaid, but inside the elevator are two new characters, Elevator Mother (Joan Blackman) and Elevator Daughter (Kirsten Bishopric). Once again, uninfected people are leafing through a magazine. If this is satire, we could regard it as an attempted comment about 'the mediated life', which could seem a rather démodé hypocrisy from a recently-underground filmmaker formed in the era of Warhol, but we must remember that he was also formed in Canada. The Canadian underground cinema was as influenced by T. S. Eliot as the American underground was by Ezra Pound, and it was bounded, as we've seen, by a snobbish official culture of Griersonian documentary. Living in such a climate, even an artist as intelligent as Cronenberg could be forgiven for thinking that it was worth mocking consumerism in a film he'd spent years trying to make because he wanted to be consumed.

The last few scenes' alternation of food, faeces and gore is followed by a fusion of food and viscera, as the delivery boy enters the elevator and on-screen space by squeezing red fondant from a pastry, his manner and its colour so reminiscent of a Romero zombie with a handful of guts that for a moment the mass in his hand seems to be both food and viscera. The delivery boy shares and extends the zombie-like quality of the Laundry Woman, and Cronenberg repeats the pattern of of point-of-view shots that preceded his infection by her. In an exterior shot from the corridor, we see the delivery boy trap both mother and daughter. Mercifully, the elevator door closes, and the rest of the attack occurs off-screen.

A single-shot scene shows Forsythe at the Guilbaults' apartment, bandaging Mrs. Guilbault's arm. The lighting is classically bright, brighter than that of Betts' apartment, and less sculptural. This seems like a humane consideration of the Guilbaults' age; they live in a bubble of age-appropriate aesthetics.

Back at the Tudors' apartment, Janine has fallen asleep. Her clasped hands and the position of her exposed legs combine body language of containment and openness. On the soundtrack, Nick calls her name, waking her. His voice has a supplicating tone, unlike the brusqueness we've so far heard from him. Janine enters the bedroom in silhouette as before. Nick is now sitting in bright light, sharing the frame with the marine planet lampshade, but now its underlying framework is more visible, returning it to the state of a domestic prop. The parasites have converted their hive, and it's clear that Nick is closer to Sviben than Laundry Woman, but more sophisticated in his approach. 'Hello darling! I feel wonderful. Come here, come and join me on the bed.' This is the longest we've heard Migicovsky's voice without post-syncing, and the usual *unheimlich* effect of a post-synchronised voice is reversed here – Migicovsky delivers his lines with an oleaginous musicality more sinister than his indifference, and not only because we know what it means.

He showers her with stilted compliments, although his use of the phrase 'the most sexy thing alive' suggests an objectification which could belong as much to the parasites as to him; that it suggests both is surely the point. Janine moves Nick's hand from her breast to her arm, revealing her unease physically before she expresses it verbally: 'Nick, you're so strange.' Again, one of the infected refers to sex as 'love', and Nick's words ('You will make love to me won't you, Janine? You're my wife') both put him in the passive role, and appeal to the authority of socially-prescribed behaviour. Like Laundry Woman's language and make-up, Nick's approach, once infected, reflects the values he already had. An ugly coerced embrace ends when Janine feels the parasites in Nick's stomach under her hand and recoils. A smooth downward tilt removes the lampshade from the frame, and for the second scene in a row, Cronenberg cuts away from the beginning of a rape.

When St. Luc arrives in the garbage room, a long shot frames the space with the same sense of geometry we saw in the lobby, tying together the materiality of the building's most and least public, prestigious zones. With the inclusion of a motorbike, production design provides a detail of characterisation for another of the film's functionally-labelled figures. As St. Luc passes through into an inner room, Garbage Room Man rises into view in the foreground as though he had been kneeling since we saw him working under the doorman's desk. We're positioned over his shoulder, seeing him as a threat yet looking alongside him. In the next room, St. Luc opens a garbage chute to reveal a prominent Sprite carton, and begins digging through the rubbish with a crowbar, finding the parasite almost immediately. Sonny Forbes gives Garbage Room Man's run across the outer room a balletic quality; we haven't seen the infection associated with physical grace before. As St. Luc examines the parasite on the end of the crowbar, the man jumps him.

During the ensuing scuffle, Cronenberg establishes the fear of homosexual rape with glimpses of the man's expressions and open shirt. As he knocks St. Luc to the floor, we see a pin-up in what we'd imagine to be an inconvenient place – it's in the dead centre of the wall, and a cardboard box overlaps it. Despite its almost abstract off-handedness, this detail confirms the polymorphous perversity of the infection, of which more will soon be made; we take it to mean that St. Luc's attacker was heterosexual before his infection. His mouth now bloodied, St. Luc grabs the crowbar. We see that, like Sviben and Nick, the man bears no outward sign of infection, but as will become more obvious in the next scene, Nick's recovered health is a fragile illusion, whereas this man is fit. The distance between St. Luc and Garbage Room Man seems to contract and expand between cuts, the distance and lighting on his set-ups changing markedly. St. Luc's panic, struggling to get up from the pile of boxes and defend himself, is vividly conveyed by Hampton.

In a low-angle shot, St. Luc brings the crowbar down on the man twice. His own mouth is streaming with blood and spittle, making him appear more grotesque than his victim, who remains out of frame. A brief insert shot shows the dead man's head covered in unnaturally scarlet blood, as St. Luc drops the crowbar next to the body. In a return to the previous low-angle set-up, we see the anguish on his face as he walks out of the frame. This is an extraordinary moment. Under the threat of rape, St. Luc has broken out of the complacency of his reaction to the attack on Forsythe, and committed murder. The almost non-sequitur quality of this scene's brutality changes the film's emphases, establishing chaos as Starliner Tower's 'new normal'.

We return to the Tudors' bedroom to find Nick's attack on Janine still ongoing. As with Hobbes' strangulation of Annabelle, Cronenberg keeps the choreography vague, representing the attack with a rolling hug. As Janine withdraws, Nick's repetition of 'make love to me' reclassifies him as one of the zombie-like among the infected. The strategic intelligence of her reply ('I wanna put my contacts in, okay, is that okay?') has a quickness new for her, and its sound contrasts with his automotive way of speaking. We see him shuddering in close up and hear a post-synchronised choking sound from the back of his throat; the collapse in his illusion of agency has been followed by a breakdown in his equally illusory physical health, and his urgency is exposed as a mere extension of the parasites'.

After Janine closes the bedroom door behind her, an elliptical cut to the bathroom shows her, to our shock, actually attempting to put her contact lenses in. She wasn't ready to escape as we'd hoped, simply stalling for time. Her failure to recognise his loss of identity makes the situation more disturbing; we appear to be watching Janine steeling herself to endure marital rape. She puts her lenses in while crying, a low-key but wince-inducing physicalisation of her emotion, combining naturalism with behavioural extremity. The scene ends on her hand clenching, a naturalistic gesture stylised into a symbol of decision by the composition of the close-up in which it appears.

24 – Nick and Janine

Another ellipsis returns Janine to the bedroom. She enters the background of a frame dominated by Nick's head in close-up, lying on his side in bed, and holds his hair and shoulder, creating a diagonal two-shot. His vacant expression and lack of response to her return indicates that he has reverted to his status as the hive of the parasites. He becomes the site for another effects set-piece, as a parasite emerges from his mouth on a stream of blood. This is more fun than we've had for several minutes, as the puppet is obviously being pushed by Migicovsky's tongue. The composition of a closer shot favours the parasite over Nick's face, cropping Migicovsky's left eye out of the frame in order to better focus our attention on the shot's primary agent. In an insert close-up, we again see a hand clenching into a fist, this time Nick's. Janine's fist clenching was a decision, but his signals a collapse. The hand's raised position in this close-up is inconsistent with the geometry of his body in the shots on either side of it; the mind which is now the body's, and the mind of the agent who put the body at the service of this other intention, are out of alignment with each other. Withdrawing from the scene, Janine puts her own fist against her mouth.

At last Janine leaves Nick, not bothering to shut the door. Her walk down the corridor is covered with a canted low-angle medium close-up. The camera movement combines a smooth backward motion with a jagged mobile framing. This is anomalous, but appears too ad hoc to be classified with the film's conscious stylistic experiments; merely a pragmatic way of covering the journey between near-identical corridors without wasting time-consuming set-ups on monotonous results, or causing the impact of what follows to be muffled by an avoidable spike in claustrophobia.

On this visit to Betts' apartment, we see Janine cross the threshold, but as before, the door is already open. The lighting sculpts Janine's figure again as it hasn't for some minutes, incorporating a subtextual 'flashback' effect into the classicism we already associate with this space. As on her last visit, Petrie is in different shots from Steele, looking at her implied position in off-screen space. Betts is now looking out on her balcony into darkness, the red shoes she's wearing standing out from her dark floral-patterned dress. Whatever view she's looking at isn't visible to Janine or to us: she appears to be facing into a pitch-black void. This suggests a different kind of consciousness from the single-minded sexual urgency we expect of the infected. As she turns around, her reaction is further slowed by a post-production process.

Cronenberg uses step-printed slow motion, a technique he'd used in *Stereo* and *Crimes of the Future*. The process entails a loss in image quality – rephotographed by an optical printer, the frames gain grain – and results in a staccato motion quite different from the smooth progression achieved by shooting at high frame-rates. It's a technique which prevents viewer immersion, as even the least technically-aware viewer can tell that this is a made image; where conventional slow motion creates the feeling of a dream or altered consciousness, step printing foregrounds the mechanical nature of motion pictures, rupturing the illusions of continuous motion and transparency upon which the illusionist cinema depends. This being an illusionist narrative film, we read this breach of illusion 'back into' representation as expression of intent. At the moment she comes into her power, Betts becomes a series of images of Barbara Steele – which, in materialist terms, is what she's been all along.

After a brief handheld check-in on St. Luc racing upstairs, we return to the lobby with a close-up of the cover of *Nurse in Arabia*, another in the Hospital Romance series of the Woman's Weekly Library. This is a female-identified book and genre; the doorman wants romance. The more conventional choice for this gag would have been something sleazier, but Cronenberg isn't looking for complicit laughs; this choice of book furthers the doorman's identification as an innocent figure. On repeat viewing it will occur to us that Shivers itself qualifies as a surreal medical romance, taking place in a sensory desert. A buzzing sound cues a frontal, near-axial cut. Heading to its source, the doorman moves into the shot's deeper space, beyond the lobby's glass wall.

Getting the elevator door open, he discovers the mother lying on the floor, looking towards him but motionless, appearing unconscious. In a two-shot, her daughter stands with the delivery boy. As the doorman backs away in long shot, and the spatial relationship of the three figures in the elevator is clarified, the shock of the man and the girl together doesn't obscure the fact that this staging upholds a taboo as grave as the one it transgresses. Having the infected mother appear incapacitated until she can follow the waiter and her daughter out of the lift is an emphatic and unsuccessful attempt to contain the implications of their previous scene. When we left them, the mother was holding her daughter and about to be infected. The most appalling scenario this suggests is that the mother, once infected, participated in the attack on the daughter. The mother's condition and her immediate focus on the doorman – we see her seeing him before we see the man and her daughter – is presented to cancel out any thought of their sexually interacting, but the image's assertion is undermined by its breach of visceral logic. We know that some victims pass out while others don't, but Cronenberg's mechanistic sensibility would usually require a rational correspondence between this variation and the relative strength of the victims' bodies. Though an adult, and the first to receive the parasite, the mother recovers last.

Discussing Sade's *Philosophy in the Boudoir* (1795), Angela Carter argued that Sade's decision to have Madame de Mistival faint while being raped by her daughter Eugénie constitutes a failure of nerve,[40] and for the moment, Cronenberg too seems to draw the line at the body of the mother. If we look at this scene in relation to the rest of the film, however, it's clear that his will to transgression excludes not only mothers, but the nuclear family as a whole. All the film's instances of paedophilia are committed by unrelated or anonymous assailants, and none of the infected children are seen to target their parents. A later scene of incest between a father and his adult daughter, though not quite depicting the same taboo, nonetheless incorporates a number of safety features, which we'll look at when we come to it.

To this extent, Cronenberg upholds Starliner's garrison mentality: the threat is Out There, beyond the front door. It was only when the director's own family structure collapsed that he was willing to make the family a site of horror; *The Brood*, the film that resulted, is the only one of his works whose horrors seem to inspire more hatred in their author than curiosity – no coherent explanation of the Raglan process is offered, and the tension reaches a pitch of raw, superstitious panic otherwise absent from his work.

In an unprecedented joint effort, the delivery boy, the daughter and the mother work together to infect the doorman, the adults holding him down for the child's kiss. At the moment of contact, Cronenberg again uses step-printed slow motion; it appears that on this occasion, only alternate frames have been repeated, a variation which, accompanied by the scene's (no longer) synchronous sound, creates a hallucinatory effect. We're spared the details of this assault by a return to the previous set-up; what we see of it matches the softness we associate with its victim.

In their apartment, the Guilbaults have started watching television (like Janine's, it remains out of frame). The tranquillised quality of Starliner living is again suggested, as Mrs. Guilbault, now recovered, looks disapprovingly at the anxious Forsythe. While the Guilbaults turn their attention to the television, Forsythe yawns and covers her leg. Cronenberg cuts to a classic crime movie insert shot, showing the telephone wires being cut. This is the most advanced thing we've seen the infected do yet, a leap forward in calculation from the zombie-like collaboration that brought about the doorman's infection. We never find out who did this, and it doesn't seem to matter. The shot is held for a beat after its action has concluded, giving us a moment to consider the will to anarchy it reveals. In the Guilbaults' apartment, a bump and a woman's laughter is heard from the corridor; this is the first time that the infection has been associated with high spirits. That we, and Forsythe, are so sure that this quite ordinary rowdiness is parasite-related is another indication of the sedated Starliner norm. In less than a minute, we've learned that the infected can work together, plan, and have fun.

25 – Forsythe decides to call the police

As Forsythe reacts, and Mrs. Guilbault reacts to her reaction, Mr. Guilbault remains oblivious, continuing to watch the television; another fearful association of television and aging. The tight framing and shot/reverse shot exchanges in this scene make this apartment seem smaller than the others we've seen, a contraction of off-screen space in the mind's eye which amplifies the threat from outside. Leaving in search of St. Luc, Forsythe ignores the distress of the Guilbaults. We know that, in existential terms, she's 'a woman who works as a nurse', not 'a nurse', but in the context of her vocation, this moment is the structural equivalent of St. Luc's murder of Garbage Room Man: he's a doctor who has killed, she's a nurse who has ceased to care. Her departure from the

Guilbaults' apartment is followed by the last of the film's stylistic one-offs.

Forsythe's run to the garbage room is covered in three handheld point-of-view shots. The sudden kinetic jolt, with its onrush of lighted textures approaching abstraction, wakes us up for the film's last stretch (we're entering the sixty-second of its eighty-seven minutes), and provides a sense of release after the previous scene's alternation of two tightly-framed, brightly-lit set-ups. Traditionally, point-of-view shots cement viewer identification, but this outbreak of formal exuberance distances us from the character whose vision it ostensibly represents, even as Forsythe's shouts of 'Roger!' on the soundtrack pull us back to the off-duty, private space she created between them before the evening's incidents. The lower region of the building will take on an expressionist quality in subsequent scenes, and these three shots, disguised as one, give concrete form to *Shivers*' plunge into the psychology of base drives and irrational states.

Cronenberg builds the eerie sense of emotional displacement in three ways. Firstly, he cuts to a tripodded low-angle shot of the garage room's threshold in anticipation of Forsythe's arrival. Secondly, he directs Lowry to a highly stylised performance of Forsythe's horror when she trips over the janitor's body. She rises wincing, then freezes her face in a mask of shock, backing towards the doorway. Her bloodied palm, held open, joins the red boxes and carrier bag hanging behind her in a formalist pattern, uniting figure and ground – or resident and building. In close-up, with her hair over her face, she backs out of the frame. Lastly, Cronenberg holds this shot until Lowry's shadow has passed from the blood-smeared, shiny black door; our attention slides to geometry, and textures of door and blood.

The geometric strength of this image continues through the next two shots, which return us to the lobby. Merrick is checking through post at night; surrounded by so many more spectacular oddities, this slightly 'off' bit of routine may bypass our conscious attention, but it creates a subliminal uncertainty. St. Luc is emphatic about the urgency of the situation, but fatally, unlike Forsythe, still trusts in the Starliner infrastructure, delegating Merrick to call the police. As Mr. Guilbault answers the internal line on the soundtrack, Merrick's shifty look back at St. Luc turns our uncertainty into suspicion; immediately, St. Luc seems naive. Learning that Forsythe left in search of him, he leaves in search of Forsythe. It's a measure of Cronenberg's invention that it's only when we see

St. Luc exit in the same set-up as he entered that we recognise the element of B-movie runaround filler in this separation-rescue interlude.

Cronenberg cuts to the film's first infected mob, who are as happy as the woman we heard laughing outside the Guilberts' apartment. They seem like the organisers of a nightmarish surprise party, approaching the door of an apartment with a demented, loping jollity; some of them moan happily through clenched teeth. Their leader's possession of a large ring of apartment keys is another demonstration of their capacity for calculated strategy. Intercut interior shots reveal the Guilbaults as their target (the second of these reuses the frames of Mr. Guilbault saying 'my wife' to Forsythe earlier, re-voicing them with 'My God!' in post-production, a drastic patching-up presumably required by mismatched mob shots rather than the tempo of the sequence). Cronenberg once again spares us a depiction of the attack itself, cutting away from the now-empty corridor.

26 – Forsythe runs into the garage

Forsythe's run into the underground car park is foleyed, each footstep re-recorded and loud in the mix. The textures of these sounds, heard over a long shot, resume the Bressonian approach we noted during Nick's rush to work. *Shivers*' soundtrack features a great deal of foley and re-recorded dialogue – Allan Migicovsky, in particular, seems to have had most of his on-set line deliveries replaced in post-production – but the separateness of sound and image is conspicuous here, where the camera distance and microphone distance differ, and in a location the film has already associated with a formalist attention to texture. The sequence that follows continues this approach to sound; we hear car noises cut and mixed like a musical score, the film's most playful soundtrack helping to build its most oppressive sequence.

A woman in a red blouse is being raped on a green car bonnet, by a man in an orange shirt. The use of colour in this sequence is more stylised than that found in the rest of the film; the three primaries, and two bright secondaries, orange and green, are set against the grey concrete of the garage. These colours enhance what details of colour the location possesses (yellow safety paint, a green-tinted light seen in passing), adding stylisation to a sequence of visceral action, in a setting which challenges any but documentary aesthetics. Once again, as at Linsky's office, we may be reminded of Jean-Luc Godard, who in his 'sixties work frequently deployed props and vehicles in primary colours to turn *plein air* shots into comic-strip panels.

The assault is cross-cut with Forsythe trying the doors of cars. Her gasps and footsteps are mixed loud on the soundtrack; Lowry's moan through clenched teeth on the soundtrack, laid over the long shot, sets up her expression as she starts the car in close-up, direction and sound editing fusing aural and visual performances. Forsythe's driving off distracts the rapist almost enough to allow his victim to escape. The yellow car leaves its frame entirely before Cronenberg cuts to a shot of it driving down the central passage of the garage. It moves slowly, the tone of its motor even, low and continuous, seeming to hamper Forsythe's escape rather than hasten it. An insert close-up of the car's back wheels shows them going over the garage shutter's sensor wire. The door doesn't open. The staccato of the mechanism, Forsythe's hand hitting the wheel in frustration, the ongoing sound of the engine and the screech of the wheels set up a rhythm.

When Forsythe pushes the car door open, a hand rides into on-screen space, tugging on the door's handle. Our awareness of off-screen space has unexpectedly coincided with our protagonist's, a surprise built upon as a handheld reverse shot, taken from the other side of the car, reveals the doorman, not the orange-shirted man we expected. During the ensuing action, Lowry's performance of Forsythe's screaming amplifies our disorientation with a sonic assault.

St. Luc's beat of remorse on recognising that Forsythe has discovered the janitor's body is a crucial grace note from Hampton. Without this confirmation of his moral agency, what he does next could become too easy to accept. As he runs through the garage to find Forsythe, Cronenberg cuts in a point-of-view shot in which we see the doorman's silhouette through the car's rear window, moving on top of Forsythe. This detail is the closest any of *Shivers*' rape scenes comes to the crassness of pure exploitation.

A close-up of Forsythe's face upside-down in the frame, loading disorientation upon disorientation, foregrounds direction and the physical limitations of a documentary-like relation of camera to staging. St. Luc's second killing takes place only a short distance from his first. Turning his face to the car's windscreen, actor Wally Martin looks directly into the camera; after so many other confrontational elements, this doesn't seem like the accident it probably was. If experienced as an intentional aesthetic jolt, it ends the sequence's worst horrors with a horribly cartoon-like implication of viewer collusion.

The shot of St. Luc lowering his gun is the only one in the film that runs slightly longer in its American release than in the Canadian original; presumably, it was assumed that Americans would want to take a moment longer to give firearms their due. The orange-shirted rapist's abandonment of his victim to see what has happened suggests that the infected not only work together, but concern themselves with each other's welfare. When St. Luc drags the guard's body out of the yellow car, the loud foley resumes the materialist, sensual depiction of cars, this time with sounds of fabric against fabric.

The orange-shirted man, cross-cut once again, gets into a blue car as Forsythe and St, Luc get into their yellow one, and a not-quite car chase begins. Although pursuer and pursued are never seen in the same shot as each other before they collide, their spatial relationships remain clear; belying his lack of experience in action staging, Cronenberg makes the outcome 'follow', in terms of screen space, pacing and the 180-degree rule. During this action, we get our first clear view of Forsythe since she was attacked. Lowry's expression mingles shocked detachment and cold determination. From this point, we're certain that 'something' has happened – but didn't we think it might have happened already, and hasn't the preceding action provided adequate realistic justification for her mood?

The pursuit of primary colours culminates in a shot of the bloodied windscreen and driver which, primed by the colour scheme to recall Godard's line on screen violence, we're prepared to see as an explosion of red – stop, danger and sex, as well as violent death. Anticipating the fuller conjunction of Cronenberg's Bressonian traits and his fascination with cars in *Crash* (1996), we could imagine this violent contact between vehicles as a sexual contact by other means, the staging of a surrealist's biological pun – one of the modes of disease transmission is *vehicle-borne* transmission. After this collision, Forsythe never returns to 'normal'. Lowry has modulated her performance through different kinds of shock; in later scenes, she moves into a different register entirely.

27 – *Crash*

It's at this point that the film itself changes tack. The last few action-packed minutes have shown us nothing that really needs to be in a horror film. Semi-realistic rapes, a deadly shooting, a car crash – we could be watching *Dirty Harry* (Don Siegel, 1971) or *Death Wish* (Michael Winner, 1974). Cronenberg has given us a brief burst of the kind of film this could have been – grittier, less conceptual – to make us more open to what the film is about to become. For now, the couple who arrive in the lobby to confront Merrick return the film's tone to social satire. The couple's performances are slightly larger than life, but only appear so when we consider them in isolation; in the context of the extreme behaviour we've just witnessed, and even set against Mlodzik's mellow but eccentric style, they seem naturalistic.

A brief cutaway to the garage confirms the change of tone. St. Luc knocks the windscreen out of its frame with a crack, like pushing an ice-cube from its tray; its bounce on the bonnet is a comical touch, in sympathy which what preceded this cutaway and follows it.

In the lobby, Merrick's sinister quality has softened into comic cageyness. 'There might be a connection, it's about your locker' (*Shivers*' only instance of the famous Canadian 'aboot'). The comic tone is developed, Mlodzik signalling Merrick's lying with outrageous broadness, as he invites the couple to come and look at 'some things that were being thrown around'. A second cutaway shows St. Luc and Forsythe clambering out of the car; as with the attack on the Guilbaults, we may feel that the action is being cross-cut to a fault, but the fatigue of our protagonists adds a crucial qualification to the comic energy of what follows.

The orgy of the infected in Merrick's office shifts the film's depiction of the infected as a whole. After the grim onslaught of the preceding reel-and-a-bit, we're relieved, a reaction which implicates us in a different way. Laundry Woman, 'hungry for love', seemed comic, but since her scene, the infected haven't been much fun. Before Merrick and the couple enter, this group's behaviour is staid, not even 'petting'. The man holding a flower and a purple nightie is the film's only depiction of paraphilia. Mlodzik gives the infected Merrick a villainous relish; the care he takes removing his jacket and unbuttoning his waistcoat is another trace of civilised proprieties in the behaviour of the infected. Alongside social satire, the director satisfies exploitation spectatorship: one of the infected is the first topless woman we've seen for twenty-three minutes.

St. Luc and Forsythe's walk back from the garage is accompanied by the melancholy flute music we heard over Janine's visit to Betts earlier. Prepared by this aural flashback, we return to Betts' apartment, where Janine is crying onto her leg, Betts shushing her maternally and stroking her hair. Again, we're surprised by both the narrative and our own reactions to it. Having taken us through suspense and black humour, either of which would be more conventional modes for this scene, Cronenberg recasts the dynamic of deception and infection in a romantic, sensual register.

28 – Betts as vampire

In medium shot, Betts' dress, Janine's skirt and the velvet cover on Betts' sofa flow together, making an island of colour, variety and texture. Betts' left hand cups Janine's rear. Moving her body beneath Janine, Betts raises her pelvis, sexualising the embrace as she asks 'Do I feel good to you?' Janine, reading nothing in either motion or question, replies 'Yes, very good.' In close-up, Betts looks at her intently. Betts' posture and expression evoke vampirism, a signal strengthened by the loose black scarf arranged around her neck in the traditional bite-concealing manner. She looks up, as though checking the time, before continuing: 'You know what I want.' In another close-up of Janine on Betts' lap, we see Betts' hand pull her hair together gently with her fingers, before continuing to stroke. In close-up again, Betts finally discloses her intention: 'I want you to make love with me.' Janine rises across the cut from another brief close-up to the medium long shot. Betts repeats 'make love to me'; again, one of the infected casts themselves in the passive role, and uses the phrase 'making love'. Where Nick repeated his words like a zombie, Betts repeats hers like an incantation. Janine replies 'You can't be saying that' but it is she who makes the first move, approaching Betts. As they kiss, Cronenberg cuts to an extreme close-up of their necks. Betts' throat bulges as Nick's stomach did. The grotesque aspect of this is immediately softened by a romantic close two-shot, before a return to extreme close-up shows the bulge appearing in Janine's throat. As Janine begins to return Betts' embrace, she takes the dominant position. We haven't seen an infection that involved less violence than this; the parasite has played Cupid, hastening something 'meant to be'.

After a brief cutaway sequence to remind us that Linsky is still *en route*, we rejoin Forsythe and St. Luc in a purgatorial corridor. Lowry gives Forsythe a carefully-modulated body language. Initially, she appears exhausted, but when St. Luc tries a door, she surrounds him in a way that seems predatory, shifting her feet, opening her mouth to show her lower teeth, and looking at him down her nose with her head tilted back. Her body, still dressed for dinner, creates a serpentine curve of blackness. Perceiving a threat in Forsythe's slow, clinging movements, we recognise that anything even fleetingly sexual is now ominous. Our unease is heightened by the vacant, indefinable look in her eye as the camera pans to follow their turn into the next corridor.

Our protagonists find refuge in a boiler room, via a clumsily-inserted close-up of Hampton's hand grabbing a door-handle. As with the flashback during Brad's examination, it's a needless reinforcement by a director making his first illusionist narrative film, and futile in any case – a shot of a door-handle grabbed but not used only increases our suspicion that these two spaces were not contiguous. In this scene, Lowry uses responsive and indifferent body language by turns. St. Luc is now affectionate, brushing Forsythe's hair away from her face, as they sit against fuse boxes in an uncomfortable-looking corner. This isn't a joke about what an inconvenient time St. Luc has picked to respond to Forsythe's interest in him – that is, it isn't *just* a joke; the association of deep emotion and physical indignity is intrinsic to this author's view of the human condition.

FOOTNOTES

40. Carter, p. 131-2.

Fifth Reel

A shot from Linsky's car repeats the sense of momentum and excitement conveyed by a similar shot of the building at the film's opening, but the geometry we see is now garbled. His 'MD on call' sign is a poignant reminder of his former authority. As Linsky gets out of the car, the frame is divided diagonally like a reversed division sign, the depth of the blackness behind him so complete that in a more old-fashioned sort of horror film, one of the infected would leap out from it to attack him. But the scene we're about to enter is both highly traditional, in terms of genre tropes, and radical in execution, presaging a new sub-genre; the framing of this shot suggests a desire both to evoke a traditional expectation and to confound it.

Linsky emerges from an elevator: now we're back to ellipses. On the soundtrack, he's surrounded by a high wind we didn't hear outside; we reflect that the building has become more inhospitable than the world from which it was intended to provide an escape. In contrast to the indication of community we saw when he left the hospital, and the busy city streets he drove through to get here, Starliner Tower now seems deserted. Entering the darkened Tudor apartment, Linsky calls out to 'Dr. St. Luc?' Silver's performance of his unnerved switch to 'Roger?' is a perfect, unselfconscious execution of a venerable horror trope. Having called him 'Rog' on the phone, and 'Saint' this morning,

29 – The unknowing investigator

Linsky's use of St. Luc's professional title suggests how little he knows of the situation, making him a classic horror movie figure – the investigator who thinks the situation is under more control than it is, and is taken by surprise.

In a handheld point-of-view shot, Linsky discovers Nick unconscious in the bedroom, upside-down in the frame. His unresponsiveness, and the long interval since we last saw him, end the scene's traditional patterns with the first instance of a distinctively Cronenbergian dread: the discovery of a body whose changed nature as *matter* has cancelled out the identity of its owner. Linsky sees motion under the bed covers, and pulls them aside. Any discussion of *Shivers* must note that *Alien* (Ridley Scott, 1979) was evidently influenced by it both technically and conceptually, and the next shot makes that most obvious: the parasites appear to have broken through Nick's stomach, and lie in a cloacal heap. As Linsky stares in horror, one of the parasites flies onto his face; their ability to leap, which seemed like a comic anomaly in retrospect, recurs now, in their most appalling appearance.

As Linsky struggles with the parasite, the racing heartbeat we heard long ago, over the struggle of Hobbes and Annabelle, once again appears on the soundtrack. Unlike Laundry Woman, Linsky's face streams with blood. The baroque chaos that ensues anticipates the coming of the 'splatter film'; its closest then-extant generic comparison is slapstick comedy. Ludicrously, Linsky somehow trips forward into Nick's midriff, attaching the entire brood of parasites to his face and leaving his glasses behind. He then staggers to the kitchen shouting 'Burning, burning!', his suit now drenched with blood. We see some red objects on the surface behind him, which a close-up reveals to be a set of pliers. When Linsky reaches for them, we notice that the fake blood on Silver's hands is the same shade of red as the pliers' handles. Here Cronenberg anticipates the abstraction which would characterise the splatter sub-genre.

In close-up Linsky pulls a parasite off of his face with a pair of pliers. This flash of ingenuity is his moment of heroism, a beacon of human intelligence in an alien situation, and we admire him for it, whatever else we think about him. At this action, Nick wakes up, in the same upside-down handheld set-up that served as a point-of-view shot when Linsky first entered the bedroom; sensing Linsky's fight against the parasites, he's looking into the now-vacant space where Linsky was.

As Linsky beats a parasite to death in the sink. Nick walks into the living room, his stomach smoking. A struggle ensues, during which Nick pulls a parasite off Linsky and puts it to his mouth, licking his lips cartoonishly. (We're supposed to read this as reconsumption, but the shadows aren't deep enough to conceal that Migicovsky doesn't ingest the object.) In close-up, Nick bludgeons Linsky to death with pliers. As in the garbage room, the composition is a low angle on the attacker, with the victim out of shot. This time, the attacker is one of the infected, and this graphic flashback to St. Luc's most savage moment implies a switch of moral perspectives; we're once again on the parasites' side. From the film's most visceral action scene, Cronenberg changes tack and foregrounds its most intellectual concerns.

30 – Forsythe tells St. Luc about her dream

Cut to an opened up over-the-shoulder shot, this time favouring Forsythe. Forsythe begins to tell St. Luc the story of her 'very disturbing' dream. 'In this dream I found myself making love to a strange man.' This line runs over a reverse shot of St. Luc listening to her, but we can read from Lowry's mouth movement that the original line – which some academic sources have inaccurately recorded as occurring in the film – was 'making love to Sigmund Freud'. When Cronenberg made the last-minute decision to change 'Sigmund Freud' to 'a strange man' in post-production, he ascended to genius. To make Freud the speaker would have been too blatant an intellectual reference, would have given us too pat a way of situating what follows, and would have implied that the film's scenario is explicable in Freudian terms, reducing its power. Martin Scorsese's description of Cronenberg's films in terms of 'Jungian culture shock'[41] is particularly apt in the case of *Shivers*; throughout the film we've noticed hints of something less rational, with less pretence to scientific thinking, than the ostensible cause-and-effect narrative has accounted for. Cronenberg is a modern, and modernist, filmmaker, and requires a solid empiricist runway for his flights of fancy, but he's a filmmaker of the irrational, of dreams that become nightmares. It is for this reason that his works of *fantastique* are closer to horror than to the science-fiction they often resemble.

With the change from 'Sigmund Freud' to 'a strange man', the dream becomes more universal, and it's a polemic dream: the man's words are her words, and her thoughts are being expressed. It happened last night, before any of the opportunities for infection we've seen. If we're committed to the cause-and-effect narrative, this is the strongest hint we've been given that she was infected before the action of the film began. If we follow the lead we're given by her monologue, this is the point at which we conclude that the antagonist of the film is Eros itself. This is the dream she had the day before she stripped for St. Luc, and reacted with irritation to his indifference. As he calls her Forsythe, perhaps her attempts to seduce him began today. This is the voice of the parasite too, but it also points to a recognition beyond Hobbes' limited imaginings. Here the film lays its cards on the table, which is why it's crucial that Freud isn't the attributed author, even in a parasite-influenced dream, of what follows.

In her dream, Forsythe was 'having trouble' with this old, dying man. Lowry's delivery of the line 'You know what I mean?' recalls her hippie roles. At this point, St. Luc begins to look concerned. She's talking quietly, intimately, only slightly insistently, but her voice is comfortably louder than the generator. We notice, perhaps for the first time, as she says 'all flesh is erotic flesh', that a reverberation has been added to her voice. 'Even dying is an act of eroticism.' Here is the fear of the mortal body – more precisely, the fear of the end of carnality. 'Talking is sexual, that breathing is sexual, even to physically exist is sexual.' This is the perception at the heart of the film, and it's a mystical vision. It concerns an inner meaning beyond material values, to which normal intellection has no access: an esoteric eroticism of the dying body, the incapacitated body, the sick body and the unattractive body as the secret meaning of everything.

Forsythe says 'I believe him' and reaches for St. Luc's face, appearing as vampiric as Betts. Just as they're about to kiss, a harsh hissing sound is laid over her voice. The hiss continues as, in close-up, a parasite begins emerging from her mouth. St. Luc knocks her out to prevent its emergence. She appears to regain consciousness almost immediately, increasing our sense of his powerlessness. St. Luc finds a rag the colour of Linsky's shirt, which he ties around her head. He half-carries her upstairs, her passivity requiring maximum physical support. An elliptical cut takes them to a utility room, the slatted crates they pass between as the camera tracks backwards, surrounding them with this artificial corridor.

31 – Nightmare logic begins

Having revealed his *sui generis* sensibility with Forsythe's monologue, Cronenberg conversely suggests a tradition: the expressionist setting echoes a sequence in *The Trial* (Orson Welles, 1962), the closest Welles came to the horror genre; when the expected jump occurs, the emergence of arms from a crate also recalls *Repulsion* (Roman Polanski, 1965). Like Welles and Polanski, Cronenberg takes us into nightmare logic: why have the infected come here? (Beyond horror, Stanley Kubrick, yet to make his own intervention in the genre, is suggested by the backward track through a symmetrical corridor, a recurring Kubrick technique.) As the mob separate them, St. Luc shouts 'Go back!' to Forsythe, still trying to help her. St. Luc runs out in a shot highlighting the crates' geometric lines. One crate's door opens, foreshortening screen space, and an implicitly nude woman presses herself against it. Forsythe and another infected woman kiss and caress each other urgently on the floor, another arm reaching out of the crate from which we're watching to grope them. The scene ends with the point-of-view of the infected.

For the third time, Cronenberg cuts to an interstitial exterior shot of the building's windows, this time running the infected's cries on the soundtrack, the wind mixed above them. A quick-cut sequence shows St. Luc running down the corridor, a door opening, and an uninfected woman staggering into the corridor with a frantic-looking man riding on her back. We're reminded of St. Luc's earlier ruthlessness as he chooses not to help her, turning aside to enter the Tudors' apartment. Since we saw Forsythe's parasite, the infected have appeared healthy; now we return to the scene of their bloodiest depiction. In two reverse shots, as though taking the information in two gulps, St. Luc sees Linsky dead on the floor, and Nick still straddling his body. As Nick rises, St. Luc fires the last bullets into him; the synthesizer sweep recurs on the soundtrack. This is the doctor's last murder.

A handheld shot on the stairs, which St. Luc is descending. Barking noises are audible on the soundtrack; St. Luc stops and looks down and out of shot. Panting, barking twin girls on a leash combine paedophilia, BDSM and roleplay in one image. An ominous detail worth noting is the invisibility of the person holding the leash, standing in the darkened room from which the girls emerge. Up to a point, this is Cronenberg's way of owning the image, but its theatricality also suggests the existence of a domestic 'backstage' space, which would require the parental figure Cronenberg won't depict. Diegetically, this means that the infected can plan and stage relatively complex erotic scenes, adding to what we know of the parasites' range of influence.

Back on the corridor, the shouts of the infected have become omnipresent. With a cut, the camera beats St. Luc to the elevator door, from which two stoned-seeming gay men emerge. Backing down the corridor, St. Luc ducks into an apartment. In a peephole-simulating point-of-view shot, the men try to persuade us: 'Hey, come on out! You wanna go to a party?' Distracted by the offscreen hubbub, they exit the frame. Another anticipatory cut puts us behind St. Luc a beat before a light comes on; another resident extends a friendly invitation: 'Have you met my daughter Erika?' As I noted earlier, this scene's depiction of incest contains a number of distancing 'safety features'. We see father and daughter in dimly-lit long shot, a wide-angle lens increasing their distance from us, while the man's close-micced voice sounds like Cronenberg doing an accent. Their appearance – a long-bearded old man and a porn-starish blonde in denim shorts – makes their blood relationship comically implausible. Their home is visibly an unoccupied apartment into which a few impersonal items of furniture have been introduced by the production: the home in which such a transgression would occur can't quite come together in the film's imagination. A last comic touch is added by St. Luc's little 'Thanks, but no thanks' nod as he leaves.

St. Luc jogs down a basement corridor slowly enough to amplify our sense of his peril. With the camera tracking ahead of him and the corridor's even lighting, his progress is further underplayed, evoking the classic nightmare experience of never running fast enough to escape our pursuers. The interior wind recurs, now an impressionistic choice, building the tension like music.

St. Luc's embattled situation – shared with whatever part of our consciousness is still fighting the infection's transformed meaning – is expressed in his struggle to open a glass door Cronenberg shoots from outside. The visual track is dominated by interior space; we see St. Luc trying to enter the exterior space we hear on the soundtrack. This confusion of exterior and interior relates to that which exists between the film audience, sitting in interior space, and the screen's illusory window into an exterior world which is not truly external, but an aid to the deeper interiority of collective meditation. St. Luc is trying to enter exclusion, not exit inclusion; this shot conveys the psychological isolation of his predicament.

Another anticipatory camera position precedes St. Luc as he heads back into the building; for the third shot in succession, we're between him and his object, but the space around him has expanded. He sidles through an arrangement of nine irregular rectangles, adding a tenth as he enters to the sound of women's echoing laughter. Their voices are a distance-micced direct recording which bears the space's acoustics, as the doctor's steps remain close-micced, post-synchronised superimpositions. The camera's angle and distance, and Hampton's line of sight, support the auditory impression of scale.

We hear the water only when we see it. With the sense of humour we now share with the film, twinkling percussion clues us in that this is not an oasis before we recognise Janine among the three women in the pool. Cronenberg cuts back to St. Luc. On repeat viewing, the rough texture of the concrete corridor beyond the glass behind him brings to mind a dream-like image, the subterranean passage to an enchanted cavern. The building has been transfigured by Cronenberg's vision: we see its concrete and glass both materially and with the eyes of fantasy: this is the alchemy of personal cinema. The exchange of shot and reverse shot begins a pattern maintained over the next six shots.

Three elegant shots combining a track, pan and tilt, pivoting on Betts and Janine in the pool watching St. Luc, who their gaze locates a short distance to the camera's right, are broken up by two functional shots in which he searches for a way out, then attempts to address the women. These shots, evidently sections of a single pan just as the shots of the women were visibly executed in a single take, are taken from the far side of the pool. The camera comes to rest with the pool's water filling two-thirds of the frame, the women looking up at St. Luc. Their stillness and that of the shot find contrast in the sixth and last shot of the pattern, an out-of-focus handheld close-up of St. Luc's frightened face, which swings to follow him as he moves away – passing back into focus – to try the door behind him.

This clash of classical beauty and documentary functionality, the best possible formal analogue for the seductive calm of the women against the agitation of the doctor, appears to have been conceived in response to the limitations of the space. Like the greatest auteurs who have essayed location-shot, low-budget *fantastique* – Allan Dwan with *Most Dangerous Man Alive* (1961), for example, or Edgar G. Ulmer with *Beyond the Time Barrier* (1960) – Cronenberg makes his compromises indivisible from his personal style.

The physical signs of the parasite have vanished. The two women facing St. Luc watch him with a stillness which implies the inevitability of a victory which will belong to them, not to it. Petrie and Steele perform this stillness in different ways. Janine seems content, friendly, neutrally welcoming; better off for her infection, no longer frightened but a source of fear, happy and self-possessed. Betts stares in erotic challenge, now freed by the triumph of the irrational to draw on Steele's occult associations, and is given one last

32 – Their victory

touch of characterisation by her brilliantly girlish hair-twiddling. The parasite's dramaturgical metamorphosis is complete; St. Luc seems to be the last person in the world still running from it.

When St. Luc gets the door open, a reverse shot shows an artificial grass bank, topped by four bare trees. St. Luc gasps, as though relieved by its undisturbed banality, and does what he should have done at least two reels ago, dashing out of the building and up the hill. At its crest, the infected meet him. This is the only point at which they behave like zombies *en masse*, emerging from the darkness in a paraphrase of Romero's *Night of the Living Dead* (1968). The private park we heard about in Merrick's introduction is beyond the production's means; what we see looks more like a golf course. In the landscape as in the residents' bodies, nature and human agency are inseparably commingled, and thus Northrop Frye's 'garrison mentality' is subverted. Figures St. Luc only recently encountered inside have headed him off; with this teleportation the film ascends to pure nightmare logic – the fugitive runs into the people he was running from, who haven't had to run to catch him.

St. Luc retreats to the pool and slams the door. Cronenberg shoots this from across the water; in deep screen space, the infected advance. A low-level, low-angle shot of St. Luc's legs next to the pool is balanced by the entrance from frame right of Betts, who grabs them. In Freud, emergence from water is birth. Being pulled into water by a woman is thus unbirth, consumption by the feminine, but Forsythe's dream transcended Freud, and Betts will receive help. As the doctor struggles and the infected swarm through the door, the third woman in the pool, unseen by St. Luc, rises and turns: she's Forsythe.

St. Luc's defeat is completed by a playful shove from Mr. Guilbault. Jung's interpretation of water becomes relevant – the unconscious, returned to in dreams, oceanic and collective, as the infected, revealed as a collective mind, now work together. At this point, Betts vanishes. Steele had informed Cronenberg that she wouldn't participate in any filming which would require the extras' presence in the water. If this decision ensured that another character would have to infect St. Luc, Steele must be regarded as Cronenberg's most important *Shivers* collaborator. Giving Forsythe the role of infecting St. Luc was as important a decision as removing Freud from her dream.

Steele's persona allows the three women to be witches, but as I noted earlier, the fact that Steele doesn't occupy the central role in the film's climax is of critical importance to what the film is saying. There have been three women among the major characters of this film. Janine was focused only upon the approval and affection of her indifferent husband; Betts was a divine, solitary presence, aware of St. Luc but connected to the outer world only through her focus on Janine. St. Luc's infection wouldn't mean enough to either of them, and the unification of the desires of the infected and their infection is the point of this moment. Nurse Forsythe, proactive and sexually liberated, attracted to St. Luc but not depending on him for her pleasure, has represented the golden mean of this film's scale of sexual and social relations. She's closest to him, and gains most from the opportunity this moment represents. Once St. Luc is in the water, it's Forsythe, the woman he overlooked, who must initiate him into the order of the infected.

Lowry's performance as the triumphant Forsythe suggests supernatural possession. While Janine and Betts seem more themselves, Forsythe reveals an unexpected self, powerful and cruelly amused. This smile is what we've wanted to see, and we exult in her victory. In optical-printer slow motion, the delivery boy pulls St. Luc from the water. This time, Cronenberg slows down the soundtrack, making St. Luc's full-immersion baptism the technique's most 'immersive' use. As Forsythe kisses St. Luc, the synthesizer sweep which has been this film's only contemporary non-diegetic cue plays again. A dissolve – the film's first – takes us back to Starliner Tower's exterior.

33 – Emergence

34 – Forsythe's victory

35 – Forsythe's hands

Cut to the garage door. Throughout this film, Cronenberg has enjoyed cutting from shots which require us to look into deep screen space, to ones of opaque, flat surfaces. This is the last such switch. We hear the engines of cars and the crackling sound of the wire – this time, the shutter's motor works, and it rises. It stops, and Eugene Cines's 'Rooms in a Museum' begins playing again. Forsythe and St. Luc are the first to drive out. Forsythe, now wearing make-up, has a flower in her hair; she lights St. Luc's cigar with a happy, flirtatious expression. This is our only look at the infected St. Luc, and he appears disappointingly unchanged, focusing his attention on driving, with only a hint of smile as he leans to receive Forsythe's light. The timing of our disappointment is exact, a first glimmer of our return to civilised values.

Janine and Betts' car follows, and Cronenberg uses our glimpse of them to achieve further characterisation. Surprisingly, Janine is the driver, resuming the malleable dynamic suggested when Janine returned Betts' kiss. Janine has a blue scarf tied around her head, suggesting that a latent bohemianism is being explored at last, and appears to be wearing a black and pink floral-patterned top or dress, its colours similar to those of the dress worn by Betts, but of a more extreme hue. Betts is once again wearing the dress she wore when she infected Janine, but now has her hair pinned up. Masculine and feminine-coded aesthetics, roles and attributes are thus mingled in both of them. Instead

36 – The happy couple

of a registration number, their car bears the logo of 'Longeuil Automobile', a last bump of low-budget-induced aesthetic wonkiness, and effectively a last example of product placement, although this firm isn't among those thanked in the credits we'll shortly see. Cronenberg returns to the joke of Erika and her father by giving them the 'sexiest' car, a little red two-seater. In the last car we see, the Guilbaults, still beaming, are being given a lift by a man we haven't seen before.

The high-angle position is resumed, now with the car park entrance in the bottom right of the frame. We see other cars passing along the road and out into off-screen space, like blood vessels in an artery. As the camera tilts back towards the body of the building, the discordant theme music of the 'Mediascope' radio news is again heard on the soundtrack. It accompanies the second dissolve of the film, which takes us from the building's steady lights to the kinetic excitement of driving in a dashboard point-of-view shot. The onrush of lights suggests the metaphoric journey into space promised by the name 'Starliner Tower'. The newsreader now serves as an intradiegetic narrator, as Merrick did in the beginning: 'The time is 5:26am.' On the soundtrack we hear a 'Sunrise Bulletin' reporting that 'a citywide wave of violent sexual assaults' have been going on since 'late last night', while on the image track, the car – our car – is crossing the St. Lawrence Bridge, heading into Montreal. There is a car in front of the one from which

37 – The departure of the infected

this shot is being taken, and we take both to represent part of the convoy of the infected. The credits have already begun, which means that we're leaving the diegesis while occupying the point-of-view of one of the infected; this is the culmination of our implication as viewers. The image track places us before the attacks begin, while the soundtrack places us after they've been happening all night. The juxtaposition is the chronological equivalent of a crane shot, lifting us away from the timeline of the narrative to take it all in at once. Cronenberg ends the film with a last bifurcation of sound and image – and a bleak parting joke. On the image track we drive into the city with the infected; on the soundtrack, 'the morning after the night before', their behaviour is restored to its initial horror. As the newsflash ends, the shot of forward motion freezes, and we're left to consider how much we've assented to.

FOOTNOTES

41. Martin Scorsese, 'Internal Metaphors, External Horror', in Drew (ed.), p. 54.